Cambridge Student Guide

KT-483-543

Shakespeare

Othello

Pamela Mason

Series Editor: Rex Gibson

CAMBRIDGE
UNIVERSITY PRESS

PUBLISHED BY THE PRESS SYNDICATE OF THE UNIVERSITY OF CAMBRIDGE
The Pitt Building, Trumpington Street, Cambridge, United Kingdom

CAMBRIDGE UNIVERSITY PRESS
The Edinburgh Building, Cambridge CB2 2RU, UK
40 West 20th Street, New York, NY 10011–4211, USA
477 Williamstown Road, Port Melbourne, VIC 3207, Australia
Ruiz de Alarcón 13, 28014 Madrid, Spain
Dock House, The Waterfront, Cape Town 8001, South Africa

http://www.cambridge.org

First published 2002
Third printing 2004

Printed in the United Kingdom at the University Press, Cambridge

Typeface Scala 9.5/12pt.   *System* QuarkXPress®

A catalogue record for this book is available from the British Library

ISBN 0 521 00811 5 paperback

Cover image: © Getty Images/PhotoDisc, Inc.

Contents

£ 2 ·k9

–3 3 /6

Introduction

In his play *Heartbreak House*, George Bernard Shaw prompts his audience to recognise something of the powerful and romantic fascination of Shakespeare's *Othello* through the character, attitude and voice of Ellie Dunn. Ellie exposes her own simplistic view, which is compounded with a touchingly naive idealism:

> I like Othello . . . I think all the part about jealousy is horrible. But dont you think it must have been a wonderful experience for Desdemona, brought up so quietly at home, to meet a man who had been out in the world doing all sorts of brave things and having terrible adventures, and yet finding something in her that made him love to sit and talk with her and tell her about them?

Since italics cannot be heard (and Shaw did not believe in using them!), a theatre audience shares, albeit briefly, Ellie's eager confusion of play and protagonist. For her, *Othello* is Othello. Ellie projects herself into the play, responds to the character as if to a real person and sustains her hero-worship long after the curtain has fallen. She empathises with Desdemona and at this point in Shaw's play Ellie is indicating her willingness to be swept off her feet. In doing so she is effectively and emphatically paying tribute to the emotional demands of Shakespeare's tragedy.

Othello kindles and fuels a compelling intensity throughout the course of its action. A reader might worry about questions of motivation or the credibility of narrative detail, but in performance there is simply no time for calm evaluation. In the central section of the play one scene grows out of another in an organic development. Suspense and anxiety ensure that an audience's hearts are engaged in an inexorable movement towards a terrifyingly inevitable outcome.

Shakespeare exploits a scheme which is conventionally called 'double time'. He blurs the distinction between a naturalistic sequence of events taking place over the course of several weeks or months and the more pressured sense of events happening within just a few days. Logic demands time for three separate voyages between Venice and Cyprus. First of all there is the flotilla that sets sail at the end of Act 1. In Act 3 Scene 2, Othello sends letters to the senate which prompt Lodovico's arrival in Act 4 Scene 1. On another level, the action begins during the night when Othello and Desdemona elope and the senators are meeting in crisis session. Consummation of the marriage is disrupted the following evening and on the third night Othello murders his wife. The seesawing alternation of dark, light, dark, light, dark contains the dramatic and symbolic action. It reflects the opposition of forces within Othello, his relationship with Desdemona, his power struggle with Iago and the contest between good and evil.

There is, however, a third timescale in that the play, taking just hours to perform, promotes a sense of near continuous, even overlapping, action. The relatively small size of the cast contributes to the intensity of its focus. It is only at the end of the performance that an audience has an opportunity to pause for reflection upon 'the pity of it'.

Commentary

Act 1 Scene 1

In the opening moments of *Othello*, Shakespeare encourages his audience to make the same fundamental mistake as every other character makes in his or her assessment of Iago. The play begins with two characters in the midst of a conversation. At the same time as members of an audience are endeavouring to interpret the context and allusive references within the dialogue, they are being tempted to establish subconsciously a preference for one character over the other. The strength of Iago's ''Sblood' is an exasperated response to the 'Tush' of a wealthy man who seems foolish. In contrasting the open invitation to judgement of 'If ever I did dream of such a matter, / Abhor me' with the weak remonstrance of 'Thou told'st me . . .' there is encouragement for an audience to feel drawn more to Iago than to Roderigo. Iago deals rapidly with an accusation of betrayal from a man who believed that the two of them shared a close friendship. Although Iago is effective in assuaging Roderigo's anxieties, with the advantage of hindsight it can be recognised that Iago will continually need to respond to the pressure of the moment in order to sustain the illusion that he is 'honest Iago'. The dramatist's priority at the beginning of the play is to establish character rather than to provide narrative. Although Othello's marriage to Desdemona is referred to in the first speech, it is a vague allusion ('this') which is not explained until nearly 100 lines have been spoken.

An audience has neither means nor reason to doubt Iago's claim that he has been unfairly refused promotion by a man who 'loving his own pride and purposes' ignored the endorsement of 'three great ones of the city'. There is scarcely time to register that the support of his three referees cannot be verified because the 'great ones' are unnamed. Iago characterises Othello through his words and deeds but he does not name him. In suggesting that Othello 'evades' advice Iago sets up a strong contrast between his own directness and a man who uses bombastic language 'horribly stuffed with epithets of war'. In addition, Iago dramatises the event through the illusion of a factual report. There is a melodramatic pause, signalled by the short line of verse 'And in conclusion', before he conveys his feeling of rejection in words which signal summary dismissal, 'Non-suits my mediators'. He perhaps indicates his own relish for performance as he acts what he attributes to Othello:

> 'Certes', says he,
> 'I have already chosen my officer.' *(lines 16–17)*

In a sense, therefore, Othello's first words in the play are spoken by Iago, which effectively distances the audience from the central character.

Iago's unflattering description of Michael Cassio creates scepticism about his character as well as the man who appointed him. Iago reveals his misogyny when describing Cassio as 'A fellow almost damned in a fair wife' for, as far as Iago is concerned, beautiful women invariably betray their husbands. Iago's use of the word 'almost' suggests that Cassio is a man on the brink of matrimony. The phrase is usually considered a loose end in Shakespeare's plotting, but arguably it might present early evidence of a perceived stability in Cassio's relationship with Bianca.

Iago presents himself as the experienced, reliable soldier who has been passed over for promotion. The job has been given to a man who has acquired 'bookish theoric' but lacks practical experience. Iago argues that he has demonstrated his commitment to Othello, whose 'eyes had seen the proof', on the field of battle. Loyalty had therefore been established by giving Othello the kind of 'ocular proof' that later in the play will be sought as evidence of Desdemona's infidelity. The acceptant way in which Iago seems to shrug off his disappointment by briefly saying ''Tis the curse of service' might well earn him credit, particularly in contrast to Roderigo's self-indulgent emotionalism. Iago's eminently reasonable response is contrasted with Roderigo's impulse to violent revenge, as expressed in 'I rather would have been his hangman'.

Iago's invitation to 'be judge yourself' includes the audience. In the opening sequence, his sensible and down-to-earth approach elicits admiration, sympathy and respect, whereas Roderigo seems merely weak and foolish. Iago's attitude is essentially pragmatic and, using generalisation about human behaviour by referring to 'others', he gives his utterances the authority of a man of the world. Crucially, he offers Roderigo and the audience the honest confession that 'In following him, I follow but myself', which makes his enigmatic statement 'I am not what I am' seem tantalisingly significant. It embodies Iago's self-proclaimed commitment to duplicity, but its circularity is ultimately frustrating for members of an audience who might initially seize on the phrase as offering clear evidence of motivation. What is more clearly claimed is that he will no longer risk the emotional pain of exposing his heart 'For daws to peck at'.

Roderigo demonstrates a re-established camaraderie by readily complying with Iago's instruction to 'call up' Brabantio. Iago issues a series of emotive imperatives, 'rouse', 'poison', 'proclaim', 'incense', 'plague', 'throw', which serve to ensure that it is Roderigo who will face the brunt of Brabantio's questioning and anger. It is to Roderigo's credit (but also further evidence of his malleability) that he readily identifies himself to Brabantio, while Iago prefers the cover of darkness to add his inflammatory description (which explains the 'this' of the play's opening speech), 'an old black ram / Is tupping your white ewe'. He does not give his name, even when questioned, but Brabantio's judgement that he is a 'profane wretch' and 'a villain' unwittingly articulates the truth that other characters will fail to recognise until very late in the play. Iago's abrupt, aggressive phrasing contrasts with Roderigo's openness and deference to the father to whose 'fair daughter' he had been an unsuccessful wooer. By dismissing Roderigo as he does, Brabantio endorses his daughter's rejection of Roderigo's courtship.

When Roderigo and Iago are once again alone on stage the latter seeks to re-establish their special relationship by discussing the political situation. The Duke of Venice is faced with taking immediate decisions to deal with the crisis of the 'Cyprus wars'. The state needs its most effective military leader. Iago acknowledges that Othello's marriage may well 'gall' the Duke but priority will be given to political expediency. Similarly, self-interest will prompt Iago to 'show out a flag and sign of love' to Othello despite the fact that he admits 'I do hate him'. To secure Roderigo's trust (and the continuation of a valuable additional income) Iago tells him where he can find Othello. Roderigo will be able to lead Brabantio and his men to the 'Sagittary'.

Brabantio will usually make his first appearance 'above' on an upper platform, and he will then re-enter at stage level. He laments the plight of fathers with daughters and he looks for support from a man whom he now judges to be 'good Roderigo'. Brabantio expresses regret at dismissing Roderigo's suit to Desdemona, 'O that you had had her!' It is at this point that Roderigo uses the knowledge that Iago had given him about Othello's whereabouts, 'I think I can discover him'.

Act 1 Scene 2

Shakespeare has held back from introducing Othello directly. The character who has generally been referred to as 'he' or 'the Moor' does not appear until nearly 200 lines of the play have passed. What has been emphasised is his separateness. Perhaps the kindest description of Othello has been as 'an extravagant and wheeling stranger / Of here and everywhere' but he has more commonly been presented in fiercely racial and derogatory terms as 'thick-lips', 'old black ram', 'Barbary horse' and 'lascivious Moor'. Othello will immediately, by his manner and bearing, counter the uncomplimentary image which has been so painstakingly constructed. His first words, ''Tis better as it is', are easy, relaxed and essentially conciliatory, but they are also words in which he is judging a situation. He rejects impulsive action in a way that is soothing and calming. Urgent reassessment of his character is demanded. Othello is not incited by Iago's allusion to 'scurvy and provoking terms' and, in flat contradiction of the attitude ascribed to him earlier, he expresses his belief that actions speak louder than words:

> My services which I have done the signiory
> Shall out-tongue his complaints.   *(lines 18–19)*

Although he introduces the idea of 'boasting' only to reject it, there is a hint of complacent confidence in himself.

Othello's whole mood in this scene is assured and controlled. Iago's suggestion that he should take evasive action meets a relaxed rebuttal:

> Not I; I must be found.
> My parts, my title, and my perfect soul
> Shall manifest me rightly.   *(lines 30–2)*

Othello asserts that he is a man at one with himself. There is no dichotomy between the outward man and his innermost being. The private man, 'my perfect soul', wears his 'title', or public function, easily. Iago's concern in this scene has been to demonstrate his loyalty through an account of how he was almost provoked into fighting on Othello's behalf. When a group is seen approaching, Iago believes that Roderigo is bringing Brabantio to confront Othello. Having set up the scene, he expects to be able to demonstrate the reliability of his advice.

Neither Iago nor the audience is prepared for Cassio's entrance here. Iago is the consummate actor, always able to adapt to the unexpected. As Othello greets Cassio as 'my lieutenant' and learns from him about the emergency meeting called by the Duke, Iago is silent. The exchange between Othello and Cassio shows the trust that exists between the two men, and the way Cassio behaves prompts rapid revision of the impression Iago had created of him in the opening scene. The reasons for the Duke's crisis meeting at which Othello is 'hotly called for' are succinctly conveyed. Despite the urgency, Othello will not be rushed. He returns to 'spend a word here in the house', giving priority to his wife. The brief exchange between Cassio and Iago reveals more than the difference in their social status. Iago's abrasively sexual description of Othello having 'boarded a land carrack' fails to prompt a similar coarseness from Cassio. His tact and reserve give nothing away but seem designed to discover just how much Iago knows about the matter. His 'I do not understand' has been interpreted as evidence that Cassio does not know of the marriage at this point in the play. However, Cassio has known where to find Othello, presumably because he 'came a-wooing' with him (Act 3 Scene 3, line 71). Othello confirms that Cassio knew of the relationship 'from first to last' (Act 3 Scene 3, line 95) and 'went between us very oft' (Act 3 Scene 3, line 99). In his conversation with Iago, Cassio demonstrates discretion rather than ignorance.

Iago tries again to establish himself as the man Othello should trust. As Brabantio enters, Iago hastily warns Othello '. . . be advised, / He comes to bad intent.' Othello, however, is unperturbed by the attempted arrest:

> Keep up your bright swords, for the dew will rust them.
>
> *(line 59)*

The authority of his command is tempered with a delicacy of language reflecting not only supreme confidence in his own military prowess but also a sensitivity and lyrical dimension to his character. He draws attention to the absurdity of Brabantio challenging him to fight when he suggests that Brabantio could better elicit respect by relying upon his 'years' rather than his 'weapons'. Othello uses theatrical imagery to express his assurance in his role:

> Were it my cue to fight, I should have known it
> Without a prompter. *(lines 83–4)*

For the theatre audience, such a reference is a reminder of the fiction of the play and serves as encouragement to take stock and evaluate the situation. Iago's expressed opinion of Othello can no longer stand, for by his words and actions Othello has shown a relaxed and impressive judgement. He is fluent and he is confident in himself and in his role in society. Brabantio is disconcerted to discover that the Duke is 'in council', but his personal sense of being wronged dominates his thinking.

Act 1 Scene 3

The opening section of the scene demonstrates the urgency of the political situation as a series of messages offers conflicting and disturbing news. Known to be a 'trusty and most valiant servitor', Montano confirms the imminence of the Turkish invasion of Cyprus. Although Othello and Brabantio enter at the same time, the Duke indicates his priorities by greeting Othello first. 'Valiant Othello' indicates the standing that Othello has in these political circles and the quality for which he is valued. Only then does the Duke greet Brabantio, somewhat distractedly, acknowledging the value of his 'counsel' and 'help'. However, Brabantio's overwhelming private tragedy takes precedence over his sense of public duty and he appeals to the Duke for remedy for his 'particular grief'. The Duke is initially sympathetic to Brabantio's situation, promising his whole-hearted support:

> Whoe'er he be that in this foul proceeding
> Hath thus beguiled your daughter of herself,
> And you of her, the bloody book of law
> You shall yourself read in the bitter letter
> After your own sense, yea, though our proper son
> Stood in your action. *(lines 65–70)*

However, his support melts away when it is clear that Brabantio is accusing Othello. The political decision to employ Othello has already been made (and was signalled by Iago in the first scene) but Othello, in speaking for himself, woos both the senators and the audience. The First Senator gives him emotive guidance as to how he should answer the question put to him:

> Did you by indirect and forcèd courses
> Subdue and poison this young maid's affections?
> Or came it by request and such fair question
> As soul to soul affordeth?   *(lines 111–14)*

At first Othello stands aloof from the invitation to plead his own case. His faith is absolute and he is prepared to stake his life upon his certain knowledge of Desdemona's love, 'let her speak of me before her father'. It is only 'till she come' that he offers to give his account of a relationship which was initiated and nurtured, albeit unwittingly, by the man who is accusing him of abduction. Brabantio's affection for him and curiosity about his life paved the way for Desdemona's love.

The Duke endorses an audience's reaction to Othello's eloquence, 'I think this tale would win my daughter too.' Although Desdemona is sensitive to the obligations she owes her father, once she confirms that her allegiance has been transferred to her husband Brabantio accepts defeat with 'I have done.' His 'heart' has been 'bruised' and he would if possible have kept Desdemona from Othello with 'all [his] heart'. Ultimately, the match will prove mortal to him. The Duke's earlier unconditional expression of support for Brabantio (lines 65–70) now gives way to generalised platitudes:

> To mourn a mischief that is past and gone
> Is the next way to draw new mischief on.   *(lines 202–3)*

His rhyming couplets convey his desire to conclude this business. His haste confirms that the state's military need of Othello outweighs any concern for placating the personal grievance of one of the senators. Brabantio is bitter, not persuaded by what he has heard, but the Duke loses no time in proceeding to the affairs of state, slipping easily and urgently into prose. The seriousness of the situation is reiterated and Othello agrees to undertake the expedition. His request for 'fit disposition' for his wife prompts the Duke to suggest that Desdemona return home. The idea is rejected by Brabantio, Othello and Desdemona. In fluently presenting her case to accompany her husband she is explicit about the physical, sexual dimension of their relationship:

> That I did love the Moor to live with him,
> My downright violence and storm of fortunes
> May trumpet to the world.　　　　　　　*(lines 244–6)*

She challenges the conventional assumption that war separates husband and wife by asking directly, 'Let me go with him.' The Duke is content for the couple to resolve the matter but Othello must leave 'tonight'. Othello shows his trust in Iago by assigning to him the care of Desdemona and the responsibility to convey any further instructions from the Duke. He also employs Iago's wife to 'attend on' Desdemona.

Act I ends as it began with a conversation between Iago and Roderigo which offers a perspective upon character and situation. Roderigo's melodramatic 'It is silliness to live, when to live is torment' is countered by Iago's vigorous self-determinism, ''Tis in ourselves that we are thus or thus.' Roderigo's emotional indulgence is opposed to Iago's reliance upon 'reason to cool our raging motions'. He denounces love as 'merely a lust of the blood and a permission of the will'. Through the strength of assertion and reiteration rather than argument, Iago is able to convince Roderigo that 'It cannot be that Desdemona should long continue her love to the Moor . . . She must change for youth'. Their dialogue is punctuated with Iago's repeated injunction that Roderigo should 'Put money in [his] purse'. Ten times he urges the financial imperative, and such is Roderigo's emotional dependency that he leaves the stage vowing 'I'll sell all my land.'

The debate makes it difficult for members of an audience to take sides. There is likely to be a resistance to the kind of cynicism expressed by Iago, but when emotion is represented by a character like Roderigo there is an undoubted attraction in Iago's resilience. Roderigo here has some of the characteristics of the dupe of romantic comedy, such as Sir Andrew Aguecheek in *Twelfth Night*, and there is potential for a good deal of humour in this scene. However, the tone shifts when Iago reminds Roderigo:

I have told thee often, and I retell thee again and again, I hate
the Moor.   *(lines 349–50)*

His disappointment in failing to get the promotion he sought is not
mentioned here. He says of his hatred for Othello, 'My cause is
hearted', and perhaps even Iago, the determinedly rational man,
admits to an intensity of emotion. His cause is of the heart and is
aimed at the heart. This complicates the critical quest to establish a
clear sense of Iago's motives. The play moves on with such rapidity
that an audience is concerned not so much with why Iago behaves as
he does but rather with what will happen.

His soliloquy, which ends the act, reveals his cynical exploitation of
Roderigo, a 'snipe' whom Iago is using for 'sport and profit'. 'I hate
the Moor' is repeated and Iago alludes to a rumour of his wife's
infidelity with Othello. He admits he does not know whether or not it
is true, but his decision that 'for mere suspicion in that kind' he will
'do as if for surety' reveals at least his consciousness of the way in
which sexual jealousy works. There remains a rigorous detachment in
his argument that challenges easy assumptions that there is an
emotional imperative at work. He begins to shape the means of a
'double knavery', involving both Othello and Cassio, and any
attribution of motive at this point in the play is less important than the
building of dramatic tension. Othello's 'free and open nature' is
juxtaposed with the ominous force of:

Hell and night
Must bring this monstrous birth to the world's light.

                                                    (lines 385–6)

Act 1: Critical review

In the play's time scheme, Act 1 marks the night of Othello and
Desdemona's elopement but it also initiates the pattern of night and
day, dark and light, black and white, which is emblematic of the
polarised debate centred upon the inter-racial marriage. The
consummation of their relationship is delayed by Othello's
commission to deal with the threatened Turkish invasion of Cyprus,
for it is Othello's military prowess that has earned him his place in
Venetian society. The rival claims on Othello made by Brabantio and
the Duke make clear the potential for conflict between the private
man and his public role. That antithesis will be expressed in terms of
the opposition of 'heart' and 'hand', with 'heart' expressing the
emotional experience of the individual and 'hand' the manners,
obligations and codes of conduct of man in society.

The offensive descriptions of Othello's physical 'otherness' signal
the potential for racial prejudice that will find expression through the
character of Brabantio. But Shakespeare enables an audience to
understand Brabantio without endorsing his attitude. For while
Desdemona's father 'loved' Othello and 'oft invited' him to his house,
he cannot accept her marriage. He feels betrayed and warns Othello
about Desdemona's capacity to deceive:

> Look to her, Moor, if thou hast eyes to see:
> She has deceived her father and may thee.
>
> *(Act 1 Scene 3, lines 288–9)*

Iago will effectively echo those words in Act 3 as part of his strategy
to exploit Othello's insecurity and arouse his jealousy:

> She did deceive her father, marrying you . . .
>
> *(Act 3 Scene 3, line 208)*

Act 1 begins and ends with conversations between Iago and Roderigo.
Although Roderigo is foolish and naive, his unrequited love makes
him vulnerable and prompts him to behave in an irrational way. He
is on stage throughout the senate scene and he embodies the

conventional suitor that an independent Desdemona has rejected. His initial accusation that Iago has betrayed his friendship creates a financial imperative for Iago to re-establish the role of trustworthy, honest friend. When Iago is with Othello he appears sincere and convincing. It is only because an audience sees Iago in different relationships that the element of malevolence is revealed and the diversity of his expressed motives denies conviction to any one of them. His uncompromising, repeated phrase 'I hate the Moor' directs attention to the centrality of Othello.

Act 2 Scene 1

Shakespeare immediately underscores the ominous mood invoked by Iago's couplet at the end of Act I. The storm that follows, like those in *King Lear* and *The Tempest*, works on a practical and a symbolic level. It does Othello's job for him and deals with the Turkish fleet. Montano warns:

> If that the Turkish fleet
> Be not ensheltered and embayed, they are drowned:
> It is impossible they bear it out.   *(lines 17–19)*

and immediately this is confirmed by a Third Gentleman:

> News, lads! Our wars are done   *(line 20)*

The external conflict has been resolved, but the storm also prefigures the discord and fragmentation to come, for the journey to Cyprus has forced a separation between Othello and Desdemona. She has travelled with Iago, while the ships carrying Cassio and Othello have been parted by 'foul and violent tempest'.

Cassio arrives and, after expressing concern for Othello's safety, he offers warm, generous commendation of Desdemona. He urges the 'men of Cyprus' to kneel to her as she enters, but her priority is for news of Othello. This is the first time that Desdemona and Emilia are seen together and although it is traditional to assume that they have a close friendship the text reveals little sense of a relationship between them. They do not talk to each other here; indeed, in discussing Emilia with Iago, Desdemona signals her distance from her: 'Alas, she has no speech'. The tension between Iago and Emilia is clear. There is an aggression and bitterness in their exchanges which contrasts with the lightness and distraction evident in Desdemona's wordplay. Emilia's retort to Iago, 'You've little cause to say so', suggests a rich subtext of which Desdemona is completely unaware and she rebukes Iago playfully, 'O fie upon thee, slanderer!' Shakespeare sets her against Emilia here, revealing Desdemona's superiority in social skills, her facility with words and her ease with men whose relationship with her husband can provide reassurance while she waits for him. There is a tetchiness between husband and wife:

EMILIA   You shall not write my praise.

IAGO   No, let me not.   *(line 115)*

When Desdemona seeks to smooth the course of the conversation
with 'What wouldst thou write of me, if thou shouldst praise me?', an
irritated Emilia is prompted to ask pointedly, 'How if fair and foolish?'
However, Desdemona's concern is with the absent Othello. She does
not know, understand or seem in any way to engage with Emilia. She
addresses Emilia directly just once:

> Do not learn of him, Emilia, though he be your husband.
>
> *(lines 158–9)*

Emilia is not expected or allowed to answer. Desdemona moves
straight on to talk to Cassio, with whom she is more at ease.

Her private conversation with Cassio is unscripted and Iago
provides a commentary that is characterised by resentful innuendo.
Desdemona had made it clear earlier that the public nature of the
scene was a strain for her:

> I am not merry, but I do beguile
>
> The thing I am by seeming otherwise   *(lines 121–2)*

Her quiet exchange with Cassio offers her a respite and presents
an audience with evidence of the trust and understanding between
them.

Having established the importance of Othello's public role in
Venice in Act I, the focus now narrows to concentrate on the private
man. He is both surprised and overjoyed, expressing 'wonder great as
my content' that Desdemona has arrived before him. After the turmoil
and uncertainty of his voyage, his emotional commitment to his
marriage is reflected in 'If it were now to die, / 'Twere now to be most
happy'. In taking Othello and Desdemona to Cyprus Shakespeare
removes them from the social structure and security of the
environment in which their love developed.

Because the storm has delivered the island from the threat of
Turkish invasion Othello can declare 'News, friends; our wars are
done' without having had to do anything. He alternates between
public announcement and private words to Desdemona. The way he

relies upon Iago to manage practical matters enables Othello to leave the stage, as he had done in the previous scene, with Desdemona.

Roderigo has been a silent witness to events and he remains to hold another conversation with Iago. The latter's improvised strategy here is to persuade his dupe that Desdemona is in love with Cassio. Iago asserts that she is sexually voracious and, although Roderigo 'cannot believe that in her', Iago manipulates him into believing that the removal of Cassio will provide him with 'a shorter journey to [his] desires'. Iago's plan is to provoke Cassio to fight as a means of engineering his 'displanting' and Roderigo proves a gullible and willing participant.

Iago's second soliloquy in the play focuses upon the way in which Desdemona provides an emotional focus for Cassio, Othello and even Iago himself. For the first time, he uses the word 'revenge' as he repeats what may be an assumed suspicion of Emilia's infidelity. The intensity of his language, 'gnaw my inwards', suggests an emotional commitment to be 'evened' with Othello 'wife for wife'. But immediately Iago retreats from the conventional revenge role he has created. Thoughts about 'failing' make him shift direction to think about provoking jealousy. But the details are imprecise: Roderigo, 'this poor trash of Venice', is remembered, notions of suspicion about Cassio and Emilia surface and the possible outcome of his actions might include making Othello 'love' him. As Iago himself acknowledges, his plan is 'but yet confused'.

Act 2 Scene 2

A Herald makes his only appearance in the play to proclaim Othello's licence for 'full liberty of feasting'. The two reasons for the revelry are to mark 'the mere perdition of the Turkish fleet' and 'the celebration of his nuptial'. What is again signalled is the potential that there is for Othello to confuse his public and private roles. In the precision of the allocated time 'from this present hour of five till the bell have told eleven' there is an implicit recognition of the need for restraint and discipline.

Act 2 Scene 3

There is a similar insistence upon restraint and discipline in Othello's instruction to Cassio to 'look you to the guard tonight' with explicit reference to 'that honourable stop'. Twice in seven lines, Othello calls him 'Michael', reflecting the trusting intimacy which links Othello, Desdemona and Cassio. Iago is mentioned but he is absent from what is primarily a private scene. Cassio's responsibility to ensure that all is kept in order has a personal dimension while his General enjoys 'the fruits', or delayed consummation, of his marriage.

Cassio is ill at ease with Iago's sexual banter and, although he initially seeks to exert an authority with 'we must to the watch', he is easily over-ruled by Iago's insistence upon the social imperative to drink with the 'Cyprus gallants'. Iago rapidly takes control. 'I pray you call them in' enables him to confide to the audience his plan to get Cassio drunk. Cassio has admitted that he has 'very poor and unhappy brains for drinking' and went further to acknowledge his 'infirmity' as his 'weakness'. Yet he succumbs to the party pressures so skilfully set up and sustained by a remarkably convivial Iago. His singing and joking stimulate an atmosphere of male camaraderie.

Although critics have traditionally been kind to Cassio, seduced perhaps by his air of education and breeding, it may be argued that he is culpable. Evidence of the ways in which he is at fault and should bear some of the responsibility for the tragedy is found in this scene. Othello quite particularly asked for personal support and Cassio has failed him. Although the weakness was acknowledged, Cassio continues to drink and there is perhaps an unattractive awareness of the advantages of rank when he points out that 'the lieutenant is to be saved before the ancient'.

Montano expresses his concern that Othello should be advised of how he is deceived in Cassio. Iago is able to excuse himself from undertaking such a task under the guise of his 'love' for Cassio. He is apparently anxious to help him overcome his 'evil'. When Roderigo's contrived fight with Cassio spills onto the stage and Montano intervenes, Cassio reacts vehemently to Montano's accusation that he is drunk. Consequently, Othello's wedding night is disturbed by a drunken brawl involving his officers. When roused to deal with the mayhem Othello is initially controlled, as he had been in his first appearance in the play when he had calmly defused the situation in which swords were drawn against him. He has to solicit information from a silent Cassio and, in addressing him as 'Michael', Othello prompts a reminder of the private exchange which had begun the scene. Cassio 'cannot speak' and on account of the seriousness of his own injury Montano nominates Iago as spokesman.

Iago exploits reticence effectively as convincing evidence of his sincerity and loyalty. Othello is provoked to respond impatiently. He becomes angry and demands to know the culprit ('Give me to know / How this foul rout began'), setting out the judgement that will follow:

> And he that is approved in this offence,
> Though he had twinned with me, both at a birth,
> Shall lose me. *(lines 192–4)*

His sentence upon Cassio is inevitable. Iago's apparently reluctant, falsely sympathetic account simply confirms Othello's conviction that Iago's 'honesty and love' have made it 'light to Cassio'. In dismissing Cassio Othello seeks to distinguish between his personal feelings for his friend and the public judgement of his lieutenant: 'Cassio, I love thee, / But never more be officer of mine.' His next line offers an explanation, even an extenuation, for this decision, 'Look if my gentle love be not raised up!' He is punishing Cassio not for having disturbed Desdemona but for failing him and he will make him 'an example'. Othello had sought to separate his public and private personae by employing Cassio to keep the watch. Arguably Othello over-reacts to the situation and over-compensates for the failure in a chain of command which is ultimately his responsibility. Although Desdemona asks 'What's the matter, dear?' Othello does not confide in her but offers reassurance, 'All's well now'. His priority is to return to the marriage bed, but he delays to tend the injured Montano himself and to send Iago to 'look with care about the town, / And silence those whom this vile brawl distracted'.

Cassio breaks his extended silence to lament his loss of 'reputation', a word he uses six times in three lines. Cassio anticipates Othello in describing reputation as 'the immortal part of myself', which contrasts vividly with Iago's judgement that it is 'an idle and most false imposition' which is 'oft got without merit and lost without deserving'. Cassio contemplates a direct approach to Othello ('I will ask him for my place again') but knows what the response will be, for 'he shall tell me I am a drunkard'. Iago adroitly suggests that Othello might be better approached through his wife, and that Cassio should 'importune her help to put you in your place again'. Cassio readily agrees: 'You advise me well'. Iago's persuasive rhetoric cannot remove Cassio's responsibility for pursuing a course of action that lacks integrity. His ambition is evident in 'I am desperate of my fortunes if they check me here', and there is a reminder of his consciousness of hierarchy in the earlier exchange between them. Iago neatly acknowledges the strength of such motivation in restoring to Cassio his title as he leaves, 'Good night, lieutenant'.

Iago's soliloquy offers an audience a shifting, complex perspective. In rejecting the role of 'villain' he ensures that an audience considers the appropriateness of such a definition. His justification for his actions is that what he has done is to 'counsel' a course of action with a 'good' outcome for Cassio. The language sets up a series of antitheses. 'Villain' is set against 'honest'; 'hell', 'devils' and 'blackest sins' are set against 'heavenly shows'. What is demonstrated is Iago's acute consciousness of how appearances can be deceptive. The consummate actor is speaking. His intervention will be to 'pour this pestilence' into Othello's ear and thereby effect the transmutation of what is white into black, 'So will I turn her virtue into pitch'. The mechanism of his plot relies upon misapprehension and false judgement. It is Desdemona's goodness which will provide 'the net / That shall enmesh them all'.

As at the end of Act 2 Roderigo again surfaces to express his sense of failure, and once again Iago must rebuild his confidence and revive his hope. Iago urges 'patience', congratulates Roderigo on the successful outcome of his attack on Cassio and suggests he 'Retire'. Alone again, Iago maps out the next steps in his strategy. These will involve getting Emilia to speak on Cassio's behalf to Desdemona, resulting in a scene between Cassio and Desdemona which Iago will ensure Othello observes. Again, Iago's sense of decision is marked by the final rhyming couplet of his soliloquy:

> Ay, that's the way:
> Dull not device by coldness and delay.   *(lines 352–3)*

Act 2: Critical review

The location shifts to Cyprus and the storm presages emotional chaos. The grouping of the main characters has changed and Cassio is given prominence. His elegant lyricism contrasts with the coarseness of Iago. Emilia appears for the first time in the play and she prompts conventional courtesy from Cassio and vehement misogyny from Iago. Desdemona's insistence upon accompanying Othello had caused him to employ Emilia but there is no evidence of any previous relationship between the two women. Desdemona's ability to sustain conversation is evidence of her social confidence, and when Othello arrives the harmony of their dovetailed dialogue is expressive of their mutual joy and commitment. Othello's shift from private words with his wife to public acknowledgement that 'our wars are done' reveals the potential that there can be for conflict between his two roles.

Iago continually needs to bolster Roderigo's confidence and so constructs a plot against Cassio. A vigorous insistence upon the supposed inevitability of Desdemona's desire for a change of sexual partner is consistent with Iago's degradation of romantic love. In his soliloquy, Iago focuses upon Desdemona as a figure capable of prompting 'love' from Cassio, Othello and even, perhaps surprisingly, from Iago himself. In speaking of his feelings, 'lust' qualifies 'love' but does not negate it. His suspicion of Emilia's infidelity with both Othello and Cassio works against assuming any clarity in his motivation and he admits his plan is 'confused'.

The Herald proclaims extensive celebration and this explains the significance of the trust that Othello places in Cassio. Iago's contrived conviviality does not remove responsibility from Cassio, who does fail Othello. The scene also demonstrates Othello's inability to reconcile the military and domestic elements in his life, for Desdemona's appearance puts pressure on him. Iago's apparent reluctance to implicate Cassio ensures that Cassio will turn to him for advice on how to restore his 'reputation'.

Iago is skilful but he is also fortunate in the way in which the pieces fall into place. Cassio contributes to his own downfall and his actions may raise questions about his strength of character. Iago's soliloquy is interrupted by a reminder of his need to attend to Roderigo, who enters injured and disheartened, complaining that 'My money is almost spent'. Iago deals with him briskly and then develops the next stage in his strategic thinking. His plans have developed in clarity for now 'Two things are to be done.'

Act 3 Scene 1

In performances of *Othello* nowadays, it is rare to see Cassio employing the Musicians and possibly even rarer for the Clown to be included. Cassio is seeking to restore harmony and he explicitly requires the music be played for the benefit of the 'general', meaning Othello. The Clown enters in response to the music and, in a series of punning exchanges, he communicates the general's instruction for the Musicians to leave. The Clown's reshaping of Cassio's question from 'Dost thou hear, mine honest friend?' to 'No, I hear not your honest friend; I hear you' might prompt thoughts about Cassio's relationship with the man who is consistently labelled honest, Iago. The Clown's punning discourse serves as a metaphor for misapprehension, and that he should be the representative of Othello's household foreshadows the misunderstanding to come. Cassio pays the Clown to persuade Emilia to speak to him, making clear that he has decided to use her as the means by which he will approach Desdemona.

Iago is surprised to find Cassio already taking steps to regain his position but he agrees to fetch Emilia. However, as he leaves she enters, presumably as a result of the Clown's encouragement. She makes it clear that Othello and Desdemona are, without any prompting from Cassio, discussing Cassio's situation. More significantly, Emilia reports Othello's continued love for Cassio and his stated commitment to 'bring [him] in' at the 'safest occasion'. However, Cassio is impatiently determined to pursue his own case and Emilia leads him offstage to enable 'some brief discourse / With Desdemon alone'.

Act 3 Scene 2

Iago successfully manages to 'draw the Moor / Out of the way'. It is ironic that Othello should leave Desdemona in order to inspect a 'fortification' for in doing so he renders himself vulnerable. He has no war to fight. The letters he sends to Venice prompt the audience to contrast the reality of the situation in Cyprus now with the prospect imagined in the confusion of news which was delivered to the Duke in Act 1 Scene 3.

Act 3 Scene 3

The longest scene in the play is pivotal. Desdemona immediately expresses her willingness to support Cassio, and she is encouraged by Emilia who believes that her husband is also worried. Once again,

Cassio shows his impatience. He makes it clear that he is not prepared to wait lest the general 'will forget my love and service' and he puts pressure upon Desdemona to intercede on his behalf. Speaking with fervour and intensity, she promises Cassio:

> If I do vow a friendship, I'll perform it
> To the last article. My lord shall never rest,
> I'll watch him tame and talk him out of patience;
> His bed shall seem a school, his board a shrift;
> I'll intermingle every thing he does
> With Cassio's suit.   *(lines 21–6)*

Just five monosyllables from Iago, 'Ha! I like not that', release the spring that will uncoil of itself. He then irritatingly refuses to explain what he means and, as in Act 2 Scene 3, his reticence arouses Othello's curiosity. The words 'steal away so guilty-like' colour Othello's response to the situation. They create uncertainty and the stirrings of suspicion in Othello.

When Desdemona takes up Cassio's cause, she is direct. She does not calculate her approach but relies upon her emotional truth, her honesty and sincerity to serve the man who is her husband's friend in the best possible way. In her purity and lack of guile lies her strength. She reminds Othello of the personal bond they have with Cassio and the debt of gratitude they owe him:

> What! Michael Cassio,
> That came a-wooing with you, and so many a time
> When I have spoke of you dispraisingly
> Hath tane your part, to have so much to do
> To bring him in?   *(lines 70–4)*

Othello's reply reveals that he has misunderstood the basis of her approach. She is neither asking for a favour nor does she want to be indulged. She argues for a course of action that she believes will be in Othello's best interest:

> Why, this is not a boon;
> 'Tis as I should entreat you wear your gloves,
> Or feed on nourishing dishes, or keep you warm,

> Or sue to you to do a peculiar profit
> To your own person. *(lines 76–80)*

Her language has a domestic frame, signalling that this is not a test of love. What she is proposing is merely a sensible course of action for his benefit and not hers. She makes it explicit that it will be quite different when she makes a claim on his love on her own behalf:

> Nay, when I have a suit
> Wherein I mean to touch your love indeed,
> It shall be full of poise and difficult weight,
> And fearful to be granted. *(lines 80–3)*

The fact that Othello does not really listen to her is indicated by the way in which he simply repeats exactly what he said before: 'I will deny thee nothing.' He is losing faith in the emotional bond with his wife. Iago's words have prompted Othello to turn in on himself.

For the first time we see him distancing himself from Desdemona:

> . . . I do beseech thee, grant me this,
> To leave me but a little to myself. *(lines 84–5)*

She complies with his request but it is central to the mechanism of Iago's strategy that Othello will not be left to himself. The technique that Iago adopts is to probe and to ask questions but then hold back from drawing conclusions. Othello's suspicions are fed on the vaguest of hints and oblique reference. It is Iago's reticence that prompts Othello to plead, 'Show me thy thought', for he is sure that 'these stops' are 'close dilations, working from the heart'. Using his own frame of reference, he assumes Iago's concern is prompted by an emotional commitment: 'thou'rt full of love and honesty'. Othello does not know and cannot know that he is dealing here, not with a close friend, but with a man who, as the audience knows, 'hates the Moor'.

In agreeing that Cassio is an apparently honest man, Iago ironically and disconcertingly offers words which are acutely pertinent to himself, 'Men should be what they seem'. His use of generalisation and, crucially, his reluctance to say very much excite Othello's curiosity. He fears to hear that which is not being spoken and he demands:

> I prithee speak to me as to thy thinkings,
> As thou dost ruminate, and give thy worst of thoughts
> The worst of words.   *(lines 132–4)*

The language indicates that the exchange is held within the context of their professional relationship. Othello attempts to order Iago to tell him, as he moves from the softened request of 'prithee speak' to the stronger imperative of 'give' before building to an emphatic climax with the absolutism of a repeated 'worst', alliteratively anticipating 'words'. Iago's response distinguishes between public and private roles, for though he is 'bound to every act of duty' he is not bound to 'utter [his] thoughts'. He is able to maintain a separation, whereas Othello's confusion of his military responsibilities and inner emotional life makes the tragedy inevitable. Othello defines himself as Iago's 'friend' and, picking up this cue, Iago argues that his concern for Othello's 'quiet' prevents him from sharing with him his 'scattering and unsure observance'. Having stimulated Othello's anxiety, Iago again uses generalisation as he talks about the importance of 'Good name in man and woman'. When Cassio earlier had been lamenting his loss of reputation Iago had dismissed such a concern, but here Iago demonstrates how he is able to take whichever side of an argument will further his own aims. Othello pleads again to know Iago's thoughts and Iago abruptly announces:

> O beware, my lord, of jealousy:
> It is the green-eyed monster which doth mock
> The meat it feeds on.   *(lines 167–9)*

He is still speaking in resolutely general terms, talking of 'That cuckold' but not explicitly relating that definition to Othello himself. Othello has said very little so far in the exchange but the reference to 'jealousy' prompts an extended denunciation of any notion that he might be susceptible. The more he protests, the more evidence there is that his mind is dwelling on the topic. He reveals his need for certainty in painstakingly reflective monosyllables, 'to be once in doubt / Is once to be resolved'. However, although he professes confidence in his wife and gives an absolute priority to decisiveness, his language signals a seesawing uncertainty:

> I'll see before I doubt; when I doubt, prove;
> And on the proof, there is no more but this:
> Away at once with love or jealousy! *(lines 192–4)*

Iago rapidly and concisely warns Othello to 'observe' Desdemona with Cassio, but then shifts ground once again to take refuge in generalisation as he suggests that the concern of Venetian wives 'Is not to leave't undone, but keep't unknown'.

In drawing attention to the codes and customs of the Venetian world, Iago has exposed the vulnerability of Othello's marriage. He has no experience with which to counter such a claim and Iago drives home his advantage by reminding Othello of Desdemona's ability to dissemble:

> She did deceive her father, marrying you;
> And when she seemed to shake and fear your looks
> She loved them most. *(lines 208–10)*

Having planted the suspicion, Iago then retreats with an apology, 'For too much loving you', as he insists that what he has spoken 'Comes from my love'. Othello's confidence has been shaken and his expressions of faith in Desdemona give way to his definition of inter-racial marriage as 'nature erring from itself'. Iago is allowed to press home his advantage by enumerating how Desdemona is different from Othello in terms of 'clime, complexion, and degree'.

After instructing Iago to leave, Othello has two lines of apparent soliloquy which reveal his regret at his marriage and his faith in Iago, whom he terms an 'honest creature'. On the Shakespearean thrust stage, entrances and exits take longer than audiences are accustomed to in modern-day picture-frame stagings, therefore allowing for this kind of sequence in which an audience can see how Iago is able to demonstrate his obedience and yet use what he overhears to drive home his advantage. In particular, Iago advises that Cassio should not be reinstated. Othello is urged to 'Note' whether Desdemona will seek to persuade him to do so. Iago, knowing what Desdemona will do, suggests that 'Much will be seen in that'.

Othello's soliloquy commends Iago's 'exceeding honesty' and laments his own marriage. His self-esteem has been damaged. He talks of being 'black', suggests he lacks fluency and reflects upon his age, 'declined / Into the vale of years'. But self-pity gives way, first to an anger that is reflected in the physicality of his language and then to a re-established sense of status as he defines himself as one of the 'great ones' who are subject to such 'destiny'. However, when Desdemona enters, Othello responds with an instinctive emotional truthfulness:

> If she be false, O then heaven mocks itself;
> I'll not believe it.   *(lines 280–1)*

Desdemona's characteristic concern for Othello's welfare is immediately apparent. Her response to his headache is to offer pain relief. She seeks to bind his head with her handkerchief, but he will not let her help him. He offers the excuse that 'Your napkin is too little.' Although there is no stage direction in either of the first printed texts of the play (see pages 59–61) one of the earliest editors, Capell, inserted the following direction:

> *He puts the handkerchief from him, and she drops it*

and most subsequent editions (including the New Cambridge) follow his guidance. However, the Oxford Complete Works offers:

> *He puts the napkin from him. It drops.*

'It drops' rather than 'she drops it' marks a significant distinction. The standard stage direction implies a degree of blame which goes beyond what the text requires here a stage direction. Emilia's later description of what happened, 'she let it drop by negligence', is Emilia's attempt to exonerate herself and cannot be taken as objective description. At the moment that the handkerchief falls to the ground, the text suggests that the responsibility for the action is Othello's and not Desdemona's, 'Your napkin is too little' and then 'Let it alone.' He commands his wife and she obeys.

The short break in the middle of the scene allows the actor playing Othello a brief respite and it also allows the handkerchief to be worked into the plot. It is at this point in the play that Emilia is able to make clear how her marital bond takes absolute priority. She is 'glad' to have found 'this napkin' because:

My wayward husband hath a hundred times
Wooed me to steal it

(lines 294–5)

She plans to have it copied 'And give't Iago'. Her half-line pause tantalisingly suggests that she may be aware that her action is, to say the least, questionable. She will soon signal her priority, 'I nothing but to please his fantasy'. With Iago's entrance husband and wife are alone on stage for the first time in the play. Iago is aggressive and accusatory: 'How now? What do you here alone?' She defensively pleads, 'Do not you chide', and seeks to trade for kinder treatment by asking what he will now give for 'that same handkerchief – 'What handkerchief?' – 'What handkerchief! / Why, that the Moor first gave to Desdemona', and she produces it, 'Look, here it is.' Iago earlier dismissed the notion that she might have any 'thing' that could entice him but now he commends her as 'A good wench!' and commands her, 'Give it me.' Again, there is no stage direction in the early texts, but editors following Rowe have inserted one. They indicate that Iago speaks *'Snatching it'*, or even *'He takes the napkin'*. Iago commands, 'Give it me', and Emilia's question then implies that she accedes to his request. She asks:

What will you do with't, that you have been so earnest
To have me filch it?

(lines 316–17)

Three lines later she asks, 'Give't me again.' But he gives her two further orders, 'Be not acknown on't' and 'Go, leave me.' She obeys and there seems no good reason to doubt that she obeyed him earlier and gave him the handkerchief willingly. Emilia is consistent in her commitment to her husband.

In soliloquy, Iago shares with the audience his plan to 'lose' the napkin in Cassio's lodging 'And let him find it'. The flimsiness of such evidence is anticipated by Iago in his simile 'light as air'. He now has the handkerchief and throughout the following sequence the audience's awareness that it is within Othello's reach contributes to the sense of Iago's improvisatory skill and manipulation. His description of Othello's apparent illness as he re-enters continues the metaphor of poisoning that Iago had introduced earlier.

Othello does not need Iago's promptings to stimulate his jealousy. He is convinced of Desdemona's infidelity:

> What sense had I of her stolen hours of lust? *(line 339)*

The balance in the dialogue has shifted, for now Iago says very little and Othello speaks at length. He delivers a rhetorical lament for the loss of his reputation. 'Farewell' is repeated four times in four lines and he concludes that 'Othello's occupation's gone.' He is on the offensive as he demands of Iago:

> Villain, be sure thou prove my love a whore *(line 360)*

and he threatens him with his 'waked wrath' if he fails. But Othello's words indicate that he has already decided Desdemona's guilt and that all he is seeking is confirmation. His vehemence also indicates his potential for violence.

Forced onto the defensive, Iago's response is to appeal to the world to 'take note' that 'To be direct and honest is not safe.' Othello desperately needs resolution of his uncertainty. Once again he demands, 'I'll have some proof', and pleads, 'Would I were satisfied!' In arguing the impossibility of enabling Othello to 'Behold her topped' Iago summons up a vision designed to exacerbate the listener's anger, using the same technique he used with Brabantio in the first scene of the play. He then offers the fiction of Cassio's alleged dream. To any rational person the insubstantial nature of such an account would be all too clear, but when Iago admits 'this was but his dream' Othello insists upon the reality of the actions which underpin it, for 'this denoted a foregone conclusion'. His irrational passion is evident as he announces that 'I'll tear her all to pieces!' The handkerchief serves as a trump card for Iago. Claiming he saw Cassio wipe his beard with it reminds the audience of its hidden presence in the scene. As Iago's confidence is bolstered by an extraordinary receptivity, he is able to put words into Othello's mouth and speak for him. 'If it be that . . .', says Othello, and Iago continues:

> If it be that, or any that was hers,
> It speaks against her with the other proofs. *(lines 441–2)*

There have been no 'other proofs' but Othello's language now delineates a ritual in which he blows his 'fond love' to heaven and urges 'black vengeance' to arise from his 'hollow cell'. To Iago's suggestion that Othello's 'mind perhaps may change', the latter reveals an implacable commitment to a 'capable and wide revenge' in lines of verse which surge and flow uninterruptedly over eight lines in an embodiment of his simile of the Pontic sea (see pages 79–80).

Despite Othello's demands for 'a living reason she's disloyal' and 'the ocular proof', he ends the scene convinced both of Desdemona's falseness and of what he must do. He has been manoeuvred into a clarity of purpose:

> I will withdraw
> To furnish me with some swift means of death
> For the fair devil.   *(lines 477–9)*

Othello now believes he is acting rationally. He and Iago have moved together. Previously Iago had refused Othello's demand to know his 'thoughts':

> You cannot, if my heart were in your hand   *(line 164)*

but, by the end of this scene, Iago kneels with Othello and pledges:

> The execution of his wit, hands, heart,
> To wronged Othello's service.   *(lines 467–8)*

Their union is sealed:

OTHELLO   Now art thou my lieutenant.
IAGO   I am your own for ever.   *(lines 479–80)*

Iago is granted the promotion he had said he wanted at the beginning of the play. If only his motivation had been so straightforward then he would surely now be satisfied, but it has become clear that Iago is driven by a malevolence that cannot be explained by reference to specific grievances.

Act 3 Scene 4
The reappearance of the Clown serves as a reminder of Cassio's plan to seek reinstatement. The insistent punning on 'lies' prompts consideration of Cassio's actions, and the expressed uncertainty of

where he 'lodges' foreshadows the revelation of his relationship with Bianca.

Contrary to received opinion, Shakespeare does not present the kind of close relationship between Desdemona and Emilia that there is in the source (see pages 61–7). Indeed there is clear evidence of the ways in which each woman's marital bond takes absolute priority over any female friendship. So when Desdemona asks Emilia, 'Where should I lose that handkerchief, Emilia?', Emilia's answer, 'I know not, madam', has seemed problematic to those intent on reading sentimental fondness, or a surrogate mother/daughter relationship, between the women. However, Emilia's behaviour is consistent with all that has gone before. She is obeying her husband as she always does. Her loyalty is to him, without question. A significant word in her response to Desdemona's question is 'madam', which demonstrates that their relationship is one in which she is employed in a subservient role.

In contrast with the rapid, impulsive and genuine way in which Desdemona greets him, 'How is't with you, my lord?', Othello's declared decision to dissemble is reflected in the deliberation of 'How do you, Desdemona?' Without hesitation, she trustingly complies with his request to 'Give me your hand.' There is an implicit contrast between her inexperience and his experience in 'It yet hath felt no age, nor known no sorrow.'

Othello reads her palm and over the course of a dozen lines 'hand' is again and again set against 'heart'. In just 12 lines there are twice as many references to 'hands' as to 'hearts', for Othello's commitment is now to the badge by which a man is known. His allegiance is now to his public persona, for 'our new heraldry is hands, not hearts'. Othello gives absolute priority to what people might think, to a rigid code of honour, and ostensibly he rejects emotion, love and all that is represented by 'heart'. Desdemona is somewhat bewildered by his intensity here, but she is deferential, persisting in her attempt to rehabilitate Cassio. Othello clumsily seeks to redirect the conversation by conjuring up a pressing need for a handkerchief. That there is a process of testing here must seem transparent to Desdemona. Intuitively, she realises that for some reason it really does matter to him, even before he invests the handkerchief with a mystical power to bolster its significance and his own sense of being the instrument of divine retribution. The loss of a handkerchief is rapidly equated with the loss of a soul, with 'such perdition / As nothing else could match.'

The history of the handkerchief extends back to Othello's mother, who was given it by an Egyptian woman:

> She told her, while she kept it,
> 'Twould make her amiable and subdue my father
> Entirely to her love; but if she lost it
> Or made a gift of it, my father's eye
> Should hold her loathèd and his spirits should hunt
> After new fancies.
>
> (lines 54–9)

The 'magic in the web of it' was designed to keep the husband happy. The account recognises the frailty of a man's faith, and the instability of the male gaze; the 'eye' can so easily 'hold her loathèd'. What is recognised here is the potential of male, not female, infidelity. But Othello spins his own web of words in which a 200-year-old sibyl used silk from worms that were sanctified. The moment might recall his wooing of Desdemona with travellers' tales, but here the mood is sinister and threatening (see pages 115–16).

Desdemona is unsettled, even frightened, by her husband's behaviour. When she insists that 'It is not lost' it is perhaps too literal a reading to condemn her for lying. If the handkerchief symbolises so much then her insistence 'I say it is not lost' is a truthful statement of her constancy and a denial of the implied culpability of having been careless with something that is so precious. Iago had suggested that Othello should delay reinstating Cassio and should note Desdemona's attitude towards him. As she tries to move the conversation away from the handkerchief, she seems unwittingly to confirm Othello's suspicions about her infidelity. Emilia recognises Othello's words and actions as evidence of jealousy, and Desdemona's confession to her of being 'most unhappy' establishes some common ground between the women. Poignantly, Emilia offers reassurance to Desdemona that her domestic scene is a familiar one:

> 'Tis not a year or two shows us a man.
> They are all but stomachs, and we all but food;
> They eat us hungerly, and when they are full,
> They belch us.
>
> (lines 97–100)

Her use of 'us', 'we', 'us', 'us' reaches out to Desdemona in an inclusive way. She does not respond.

Cassio and Iago re-enter and, encouraged by Iago, Cassio presses Desdemona once again for help in regaining his position. She expresses no hint of resentment to him but apologises for her lack of success, urging him to be patient:

> What I can do, I will; and more I will
> Than for myself I dare.   *(lines 124–5)*

In conversation with Emilia she rapidly finds excuse and explanation for Othello's behaviour by assuming that he is finding difficulties in his public role, and she is acutely critical of the way in which she feels she had indicted him falsely. Emilia returns to her earlier speculation that Othello was motivated by jealousy and she echoes her husband's metaphor as she speaks of 'a monster / Begot upon itself, born on itself'. As Desdemona and Emilia leave, telling Cassio to 'walk here about', Bianca enters the play for the first time. It is a brief theatrical opportunity to link the women in the audience's mind by exploiting the long entrances and exits that were characteristic of Jacobean theatre. The need to sustain continuous action would allow the three women possibly to pass each other but certainly to be on stage at the same time.

Cassio is carefully stage-managing his campaign and his strategy does not include Bianca. He is initially aggressive when Bianca enters: 'What make you from home?' The word 'home' could imply a domestic dimension to their relationship and might indicate that it is an established one. Cassio rapidly softens his sharpness with expressed concern, flattery and excuse. Bianca accuses him of neglecting her, 'What! Keep a week away?' Again he apologises and makes a further unsatisfactory excuse. He promises to make it up to her and then curtly commands 'Take me this work out' as he gives her the handkerchief to copy.

Bianca sees the handkerchief, 'some token from a newer friend', as evidence of infidelity and in a sense she is right. Cassio has neglected her to spend time with other women (Emilia and Desdemona) and, as he admits, the napkin is not his; he found it, but before it is demanded he would 'have it copied'. He again orders Bianca, 'Take it and do't, and leave me for this time.' He uses her and dismisses her. It is the pattern of male behaviour that has been established earlier by Othello and Iago to Desdemona and Emilia. But Bianca questions this command, 'Leave you? Wherefore?' The reason is clear. Cassio is a man who is concerned above all with his 'reputation':

> I do attend here on the general;
> And think it no addition, nor my wish,
> To have him see me womaned.   *(lines 187–9)*

Bianca might not be as easy to manipulate as a wife but nor is she free from the bond of commitment born of love. She craves some time with him, 'I pray you, bring me on the way a little'. Their sexual relationship is made explicit when Bianca implores Cassio to 'say if I shall see you soon at night', but there is also evidence that their relationship must be concealed. Cassio is ashamed of her and he has other priorities. The most he offers is to accompany her 'a little way' and 'I'll see you soon'. Bianca recognises that she has no power in the relationship and accepts the terms offered: ''Tis very good; I must be circumstanced.'

Act 3: Critical review

Act 3 is long and complex. It does not have the patterned structure of the previous acts and the action develops in an organic and increasingly rapid way.

Cassio's decision to employ the Musicians and the Clown reflects the indirect nature of his strategy to regain his job. He engages both Emilia and Desdemona on his behalf but he will not speak to Othello himself. Desdemona is commendably open in the way she encourages Othello to reinstate Cassio. She demonstrates her concern to heal the rift between her husband and his friend.

To encourage Othello's uncertainty Iago exploits the history that binds Othello, Desdemona and Cassio. The process of temptation succeeds because Othello is predisposed to jealousy. His sense of self is fragile and doubt generates its own energy to grow into conviction. Iago is able to exploit society's intolerance of behaviour which challenges conventional attitudes. The marriage between Othello and Desdemona is so extraordinary that it is vulnerable to Iago's innuendo.

Iago has shaken Othello's faith in the strength of his love for Desdemona. Othello reveals in soliloquy how rapidly he has convinced himself of Desdemona's infidelity, and yet when she re-enters he will 'not believe' she is false. As Emilia retrieves the discarded handkerchief her only soliloquy in the play provides insight into her anxiety to please her husband. The two marriages are connected through the transfer of the love-token. In the same way as Desdemona is steadfast in her love, Emilia's commitment to her husband makes obedience to him her priority. Once Iago has the handkerchief in his possession he is able to weave a wholly fictional account that implicates Cassio. Although Othello had demanded 'ocular proof', it is significantly on less than the flimsiest of evidence that he convinces himself of Desdemona's infidelity and decides to 'chop her into messes'.

The final scene of the act recalls its opening as Desdemona uses the Clown as messenger to Cassio. Emilia silently observes the first breakdown in communication between Othello and Desdemona. Emilia could reveal the whereabouts of the missing handkerchief but she has a higher loyalty in her love for her husband. Cassio again puts pressure on Desdemona to help him. The juxtaposition of Desdemona and Emilia leaving the stage with the moment when Bianca enters for the first time in the play might prompt an audience to recognise how Cassio exploits all three women. The priority he gives to re-establishing his social and military position makes him unwilling to be seen with Bianca. Despite her anxiety to be reassured that he loves her, she aligns herself with both Desdemona and Emilia in her tenacious commitment to the man she loves.

Act 4 Scene 1

Othello and Iago enter together in conversation, which is emblematic of their mutual dependence. The opening exchanges indicate how Othello follows Iago's lead. Three times Iago's words are echoed by Othello: 'Think so'; 'kiss'; 'Naked'. Using the same devices that were so successful in Act 3 Scene 3, Iago stimulates Othello to imagine the physical act of infidelity before returning to the flimsy substance of the handkerchief to secure the link between it and Desdemona's honour. Just as Cassio's invented dream had been recounted Iago constructs a report of what Cassio said. Iago gets no further than saying that Cassio did 'Lie' when Othello interrupts to ask 'With her?', and the casual yet graphic response, 'With her, on her, what you will', causes Othello to lose his tenuous self-control. He is not allowed the dignity of madness that Hamlet and Lear share. Othello's tortured imaginings of 'Lie with her? Lie on her?' culminate in what appears to be an epileptic fit. He is literally and metaphorically at his lowest, writhing on the ground with Iago in the ascendant.

Iago would seem to relish this moment of triumph as he urges ironically, 'Work on, / My medicine, work!' He relates the current situation to one in which 'credulous fools are caught' and 'worthy and chaste dames . . . meet reproach'. With Cassio's entrance there is a stage picture which embodies their rivalry. There is some tension as Cassio's instruction to 'Rub him about the temples' is rebuffed by Iago's 'No, forbear.' It is a moment which recalls the intimacy between Othello and Cassio earlier in the play and emphasises how Iago has replaced him. Cassio does what he is told and leaves. As Othello recovers, Iago's expression of concern, 'Have you not hurt your head?', has a veiled allusion to the cuckold's horns and therefore reminds Othello of his wife's alleged adultery. He sees himself as 'A hornèd man' and Iago assures him that his case is a familiar one. Iago then suggests that Othello should 'encave' himself in order that he might 'mark' Cassio as Iago makes 'him tell the tale anew' of his relationship with Desdemona.

Although Bianca is described in the Folio list of characters as a 'courtesan' most modern editors prefer the title of 'mistress to Cassio', incidentally acknowledging the fidelity of her relationship. Iago certainly recognises that aspect of the relationship. As well as her economic dependence, there is an emotional one. She is:

> A housewife that by selling her desires
> Buys herself bread and clothes. It is a creature
> That dotes on Cassio; as 'tis the strumpet's plague
> To beguile many and be beguiled by one.　　　　*(lines 92–5)*

In conducting a conversation with Cassio which is designed to persuade Othello of Desdemona's infidelity, Iago exploits his sense of Bianca's dependence, 'She gives it out that you shall marry her.' Cassio laughs before commenting:

> I marry her? What! A customer! I prithee, bear some charity to
> my wit. Do not think it so unwholesome. Ha, ha, ha!
> 　　　　　　　　　　　　　　　　　　　　　　　　*(lines 117–18)*

A few lines later he confirms the truth of the report, and yet he continues to deride the woman who he acknowledges loves him:

> This is the monkey's own giving out. She is persuaded I will
> marry her out of her own love and flattery, not out of my
> promise.　　　　　　　　　　　　　　　　　　*(lines 124–6)*

Cassio is dismissive and contemptuous of the affection of a woman to whom he has made promises and given instructions. He continues his offensive description of her attentions:

> She haunts me in every place. I was the other day talking on
> the sea-bank with certain Venetians, and thither comes this
> bauble and, by this hand, falls me thus about my neck.
> . . .
> So hangs and lolls and weeps upon me, so hales and pulls me.
> Ha, ha, ha!　　　　　　　　　　　　　*(lines 128–31; 134–5)*

While undoubtedly the primary focus of attention at this moment is the effect on Othello of what he overhears, Shakespeare's investment in the character of Bianca makes Cassio's words objectionable. Her entrance at this point only momentarily confirms Cassio's accusation that she 'haunts' him because she hurls his words back at him in defiance of his ill-treatment. She is particularly resentful of him asking her to 'take out the work' and copy the handkerchief. She returns it angrily and defiantly, clear in her accusation that he has been unfaithful to her. The woman Cassio has just described as a 'monkey' and a 'bauble' is now addressed as 'sweet Bianca' and, like the other women in the play, she is held by an emotional commitment and she cannot sever the bond:

> If you'll come to supper tonight, you may. If you will not,
> come when you are next prepared for.   *(lines 152–3)*

Cassio pursues her, concerned not for her but for his reputation ('She'll rail in the streets else') and, although he had told Iago earlier 'I must leave her company', he now confirms that he intends to visit her for supper.

Although Othello is hiding during this section of the scene, Shakespeare has him punctuate the conversations with comments which indicate his pressure of feeling and how he now regards Cassio as the man who has humiliated him. Cassio's laughter at the assertion of Bianca's love for him is interpreted by Othello as galling evidence of Cassio rejoicing in his triumph with Desdemona. As Cassio leaves, Othello's first words to Iago are 'How shall I murder him, Iago?' The handkerchief is no longer of primary concern to Othello, but he asks Iago 'Was that mine?' It prompts a reference to 'the foolish woman your wife', which complicates Othello's response. He is torn by the resurgence of his love for Desdemona. He cannot stop himself reiterating her virtues, despite Iago urging 'you must forget that' and 'Nay, that's not your way.' Othello repeatedly laments 'the pity of it', but he is shocked out of this self-indulgent mood by the suggestion that his fondness for his wife should prompt him to give her 'patent to offend'. Iago reminds Othello of the way in which the behaviour attributed to her has most crucially abused Othello's honour.

The determination to 'chop her into messes' is brutal, but Othello then favours poison until Iago suggests that he should 'strangle her in her bed, even the bed she hath contaminated'. Othello seizes upon the apparent 'justice' of the suggestion and the idea will inform his attitude in the final scene in the play. Iago commits himself to take care of Cassio. Their conversation is interrupted by a trumpet call, which Iago correctly identifies as 'something from Venice', and Lodovico enters with Desdemona. While Othello reads the Duke's letter, Desdemona talks to Lodovico. Othello intrudes on their conversation in a manner remarkably similar to the kind of commentary he had offered when overhearing the conversation between Iago and Cassio in the previous scene. Indeed, Desdemona seems unwittingly to provoke such a connection as she tells Lodovico of her wish that the division between Othello and Cassio might be healed 'for the love I bear to Cassio'. The letter commands Othello back to Venice, appointing Cassio as his replacement. Desdemona's 'I am glad on't' provokes Othello into further anger, which results in him hitting her. Such unexpected, unwarranted violence against a woman makes this a moment in the theatre which perhaps is just as shocking now as it was to the original audiences. Desdemona's statement 'I have not deserved this' is further evidence of the strength that there is in a character who is often, unfairly, judged to be weak.

There is a terrifying callousness in the way Othello treats Desdemona in front of Lodovico. When he urges Othello to 'call her back' Othello not only does so but uses the demonstration of Desdemona's obedience to exemplify what he sees as her inconstancy, 'she can turn, and turn'. Shakespeare seems to be acutely aware of the way in which men justify their accusations of feminine duplicity by citing women's tears not as evidence of truthful emotion but rather as testimony to an ability to dissemble. Othello alludes to the notorious notion of crocodile tears, and he describes Desdemona's distress as 'well-painted passion'. To Othello, everything conspires to confirm the truth of his conviction of Desdemona's guilt. He sees further indignity in the message that Lodovico has brought:

> I obey the mandate,
> And will return to Venice. . . .
> Cassio shall have my place.   *(lines 250–2)*

Othello's perception is that Cassio has supplanted him both in his public life and in his private life.

Left on stage with Iago, Lodovico draws attention to the change in Othello:

> Is this the noble Moor whom our full senate
> Call all-in-all sufficient? Is this the nature
> Whom passion could not shake? Whose solid virtue

> The shot of accident nor dart of chance
> Could neither graze nor pierce? *(lines 255–9)*

Although Lodovico strives to find an explanation, Iago insists 'He's that he is' and hints that the violence that has just been witnessed is not unusual. Iago again adopts the persona of one who is anxious to be honest, loyal and caring to the man he serves. He suggests that Lodovico should 'mark' Othello and draw conclusions himself so that Iago 'may save [his] speech'. There is an emphatic irony in the exit line Lodovico speaks to Iago, 'I am sorry that I am deceived in him.'

Act 4 Scene 2

The scene begins with Othello questioning Emilia about Desdemona's behaviour, insisting that there must be evidence of her infidelity. His suggestions of intrigue are categorically denied in a series of curt responses which develop into a thrice repeated 'Never'. In affirming her willingness to 'lay down' her soul in any wager to prove Desdemona's honesty, Emilia foreshadows her selfless courage in the final scene of the play. She warns Othello against the innuendo of 'any wretch' but Othello orders her to send Desdemona to him. He dismisses her as a 'simple bawd' and in the next line completes his description of the two women by defining his wife as a 'subtle whore'.

Desdemona's short questions indicate her fear and apprehension. She goes down on her knees to beg clarification from her husband, asking him 'what doth your speech import?' Her statement that she is his 'true and loyal wife' is opposed by Othello's description of her as 'false as hell'. His anger gives way to tears and Desdemona expresses her hope that she is not the cause. She asks whether he blames her father for being summoned back to Venice but urges him not to implicate her, reminding him that if he has 'lost' Brabantio then she has 'lost him too'. Her assertion of her commitment to her husband provides a reminder of how in marrying Othello she severed her bond with her father.

But Othello seems not to hear her words. His 18-line speech functions almost like a soliloquy. He reflects upon how he could have responded to a trial of illness, shame, poverty or captivity by finding 'in some place of my soul / A drop of patience'. He offers an extended metaphor which contrasts 'The fountain from the which my current runs' with 'a cistern for foul toads / To knot and gender in!' His series of antithetical descriptions demonstrate the agony that results from simultaneously acknowledging Desdemona's beauty and being revolted by her corruption. He invokes images of flies in a slaughter-house, of a weed that smells so sweet and of a 'fair paper . . . / Made to write 'whore' upon'. Again and again he labels her 'strumpet' and 'whore'. Despite her insistence upon her innocence he leaves saying:

> I took you for that cunning whore of Venice
> That married with Othello.   *(lines 88–9)*

Othello makes explicit the sense of having visited a brothel by informing Emilia that 'We have done our course' and by paying her: 'there's money for your pains'.

The brief exchange between Desdemona and Emilia which follows has an almost dream-like quality. Desdemona cannot engage with Emilia's practical questions for, as she says, 'answers have I none'. She asks that Emilia put the wedding sheets on the bed and call Iago. Desdemona has her only soliloquy in the play at this point. In three lines she seems to accept that it is appropriate that she should be used in this manner but she then questions what she has done to prompt such behaviour. Shakespeare invests her with a psychological truth in the way she responds with shock and incomprehension to her husband's violent abuse.

When Iago and Emilia enter it is Iago who asks, as Emilia had done, 'What is the matter, lady?' Emilia gives her husband an account of Othello's treatment of Desdemona, focusing in particular upon Othello calling her 'whore'. Emilia then develops the suspicion she had voiced earlier that 'some eternal villain' has 'devised this slander'. Her speculation is both astute and precise. She suggests that the motive may be to 'get some office' and although Desdemona's response is to implore that 'heaven pardon him', Emilia is uncompromising in her judgement:

> A halter pardon him and hell gnaw his bones!   *(line 135)*

She grows increasingly assured and impassioned as she argues:

> The Moor's abused by some most villainous knave,
> Some base notorious knave, some scurvy fellow.   *(lines 138–9)*

Iago seeks to silence her but she turns her attack upon him as she suggests that he had been subject to a similar experience, falsely suspecting a relationship between her and Othello. The irony is acute and the exchange makes it absolutely clear that Emilia has no suspicion whatsoever of her husband's villainy.

Desdemona implores 'good Iago' for advice about how to regain Othello's love. The text makes it clear that she kneels to affirm 'by this light of heaven' that she does 'love him dearly'. Iago, 'Good Iago', her 'good friend' is her witness. The irony is intensified as the stage picture recalls the end of Act 3 Scene 3, when the bond between Iago and Othello was sealed 'by yond marble heaven'. Desdemona declares her deep and unconditional love for her husband. Come what may she will continue to 'love him dearly':

> Unkindness may do much,
> And his unkindness may defeat my life,
> But never taint my love.
>
> *(lines 158–60)*

Iago is brusque, suggesting that it is state matters which concern Othello.

Roderigo re-enters the play. He has not been seen since the end of Act 2 and now he attacks Iago directly: 'I do not find that thou deal'st justly with me'. He believes that he has been exploited with no prospect of achieving Desdemona. He is aware that he has 'foolishly suffered' and that he has wasted his money and his jewels. Since Iago had told him that he had delivered the jewels to her and that she had promised a response, Roderigo has determined to ask for the return of his jewels and he will abandon his pursuit of her. He is also prepared to challenge Iago directly and 'seek satisfaction'.

Roderigo reveals that there is more to him than the foolish, naive gull that he has seemed. Iago acknowledges this change and admits 'I see there's mettle in thee', says he admires him more and offers his hand in a gesture of equality and respect. He improvises a plan which he says will allow Roderigo to demonstrate his 'purpose, courage, and valour'. Iago tells Roderigo that Cassio has been appointed to replace Othello in Cyprus and that Othello is being sent to Mauritania. He will take Desdemona with him and so Roderigo will lose her. It is necessary that Othello be detained in Cyprus which requires 'the removing of Cassio'. Iago has to spell out the euphemism to Roderigo ('knocking out his brains') before rapidly developing his plot and determining matters such as the location and time of an attack upon Cassio. He assures Roderigo that he will be 'near to second [his] attempt'. Roderigo requires 'further reason' and the two men leave with Iago promising that he will satisfy him.

Act 4 Scene 3

The scene opens with a contrast between Othello's courtesy in offering to walk with Lodovico and his curt instructions to Desdemona to go to bed and dismiss Emilia. It is in this scene, usually known as the 'willow scene', that critical and theatrical sentimentality in the interpretation of the Desdemona/Emilia relationship is rife. The two women have moved closer to each other, but a degree of cautious reserve remains. Their dialogue is punctuated by commands which reiterate the hierarchical relationship in which Desdemona characteristically gives orders, such as 'unpin me here' and 'Prithee, hie thee'. She reaches back in time to try to find some remnants of her past which might help her make sense of the present. She remembers her mother and her mother's maid:

> She was in love, and he she loved proved mad
> And did forsake her.   *(lines 26–7)*

It is with Barbary, her mother's maid, that Desdemona has a greater emotional empathy. She is seeking to establish a bond which eases her anxiety at her own marital discord. Seeking comfort in this way is an understandable impulse but it also suggests the lack of emotional support offered by Emilia. It seems unduly wishful thinking to see the relationship between Desdemona and Emilia patterned in the women from Desdemona's past. On the contrary, her memories remind an audience of these women's separate histories. As Desdemona echoes Barbary and reaches out to her mother, she excludes Emilia.

Once Desdemona's preparations for bed are complete, she dismisses Emilia abruptly, 'So get thee gone; good night.' Desdemona is obeying her husband's instructions that were designed to separate the women, 'Dismiss your attendant there. Look't be done.' However, either Emilia is reluctant to go or Desdemona's words delay her. Their conversation still does not come easily but Desdemona asks a direct, intensely personal question, 'Wouldst thou do such a deed for all the world?', which draws a forthright and challenging response from Emilia, 'Why, would not you?' For the first time there is an equality of discourse between them. The tension is relaxed by Emilia's joke about not doing it 'by this heavenly light' but in the dark. Her views are more than merely worldly wise. The essence of her reasoning is that she professes a willingness for self-sacrifice, not to achieve personal gain but for the benefit of her husband's prospects, 'I should venture purgatory for't.' She has indeed done as much in her willingness to lie to obey his command, 'Be not acknown on't' (Act 3 Scene 3, line 320). Emilia provides a reminder of the insistent pressures of ambition and promotion in the play. Like Desdemona and Bianca, she is consistently supportive of the man she loves.

Emilia talks essentially from her experience, and Desdemona's response is not so much evidence of childlike naivety as a further reminder of the difference of the worlds they inhabit. There is no significant meeting of minds here, though this is the closest they get to intimacy in the play. Emilia's shift into verse effectively heightens what is a remarkable speech. She is not so much arguing for sexual freedom for women as revealing a subtext of frustration, pain and unhappiness. She offers a committed analysis of the double standard that applies in matters of sexual relations. If men are unfaithful as a result of 'affection', in quest of 'sport' or out of 'frailty', then on behalf of women she asks:

> And have not we affections,
> Desires for sport, and frailty, as men have?   *(lines 96–7)*

She is pleading for equality and mutual respect in marriage:

> Then let them use us well; else let them know
> The ills we do, their ills instruct us so.   *(lines 98–9)*

Audiences understand the depth of Emilia's commitment, but Desdemona does not. This is not because she is stupid or insensitive but sadly, indeed tragically, she cannot relate her situation to that of Emilia. Rather than recognise the parallels, Desdemona does as her husband bade her and dismisses her attendant: 'Good night, good night'. Her prayer-like couplet conveys a touching faith.

Act 4: Critical review

Iago cunningly feeds an imagination which can create the reality of what it fears. Prompted by the layered meanings of 'lie', Othello loses both physical and mental control and collapses. He has lost his personal dignity and the man who once had exerted quiet authority over others is now reduced to an incoherent figure lying on the stage. The tableau of Iago's superiority is interrupted by Cassio, enabling Iago to contrive that Othello will overhear Cassio talking of a relationship. The conversation is about Bianca but Othello believes it is Desdemona who is being disparaged. Iago's staged scene works, not least because of Cassio's readiness to boast of his sexual appeal and to talk in impersonal terms of the woman who he knows loves him. The inequality in the relationship between Bianca and Cassio is evident. She cares for him, while his priority is for his reputation.

It is the fate of all three women in the play to be condemned as prostitutes. Iago talks to Cassio about Bianca and Othello thinks they are discussing Desdemona. In front of Lodovico, Othello strikes his wife, depicting her tears as 'well-painted passion'. In the next scene, he judges Emilia to be 'a simple bawd' and his following encounter with Desdemona enacts a man's visit to a brothel as he tells her, 'I took you for that cunning whore of Venice'.

In conversation with Emilia and then Iago, Desdemona demonstrates the constancy and selflessness of her love for Othello. Emilia's suspicion that there is 'some most villainous knave' is painfully ironic but it serves to emphasise that no one suspects Iago, not even his wife. However, after a long absence from the play (he was last seen in Act 2 Scene 3), Roderigo now presents a challenge to Iago who has to work hard to dissuade him from abandoning his campaign to gain Desdemona. No longer does an easily satisfied Roderigo go willingly. He requires 'further reason' for the plan to kill Cassio.

The 'willow scene' offers Desdemona and Emilia an unfulfilled opportunity for mutual support. Their physical closeness and the confidences they share as Desdemona gets ready for bed are constrained by the priority of each woman's obedience to her husband. Their marital loyalties divide them.

Act 5 Scene 1

Iago directs Roderigo to be ready to attack Cassio when he enters. He places him 'behind this bulk', which may well have been behind one of the pillars that supported the canopy in Shakespeare's theatre. Roderigo is uncertain and nervous. In contrast, Iago's thoughts upon the situation are callous. Whether Cassio, Roderigo or both men are killed does not matter to him, for any of those outcomes would equally serve his purpose. However, on further reflection he is convinced of the need for both men to die. If Roderigo were to live, Iago would be called to account for the money and jewels he has not passed on to Desdemona. In considering Cassio, Iago gives priority to a more personal envy, suggesting that Cassio 'hath a daily beauty in his life / That makes me ugly' before acknowledging that it would be dangerous if Othello were to discuss matters with Cassio.

Roderigo's attack on Cassio fails because Cassio's coat is 'better' than he thinks and Cassio wounds Roderigo. Iago then wounds Cassio. So Roderigo and Cassio both lie wounded on the stage. Iago leaves and Othello enters. It may be that when the play was presented in Shakespeare's own theatre, Othello entered on the upper level. It is certainly a difficult moment to manage realistically in performance and modern productions frequently cut it completely. Hearing Cassio's cries, Othello assumes that Iago has fulfilled his commitment to kill Cassio. Othello believes that Iago 'teachest' him and he announces his determination to follow his example. Defining Desdemona once again as a 'Strumpet', he exits on a terrifyingly graphic couplet:

> Forth of my heart those charms, thine eyes, are blotted;
> Thy bed, lust-stained, shall with lust's blood be spotted.
>
> *(lines 35–6)*

Lodovico and Gratiano enter but are fearful about the cries for help they hear and desire more assistance. Iago enters and plays the role of an innocent, going first to help Cassio, and then moving rapidly to stab Roderigo. What seem at this point to be dying words accurately identify the truth of the situation: 'O damned Iago! O inhuman dog!' Roderigo will survive and bear testimony against his attacker. As Lodovico and Gratiano come forward Iago only sees Lodovico, sustaining the impression of darkness in a scene which would have been originally presented in daylight. Iago convincingly maintains the appearance of being the concerned friend to Cassio, even calling him 'brother' and using his own shirt to bind his injured leg.

Bianca's concern for Cassio is evident when she enters, reiterating his name on seeing him hurt. Iago repeats that condemnation which is used of all three women, 'O notable strumpet', and he cynically projects his own guilt onto Bianca. His public pronouncement articulates the prevalent male attitude:

> Gentlemen all, I do suspect this trash
> To be a party in this injury. *(lines 85–6)*

Iago bustles about, calling for a garter, a chair, and effectively presents a display of innocent distress as he discovers the body of his 'friend' and 'dear countryman', Roderigo. Iago now apologises for not having noticed Gratiano's presence. Having arranged Cassio's removal in a chair, Iago promises the services of Othello's surgeon and brushes aside Bianca. Her paleness, undoubted evidence of her concern, is subject to male scrutiny, which interprets her appearance as evidence of her guilt. The repeated use of 'gentlemen' points the irony:

> Stay you, good gentlemen. Look you pale, mistress?
> Do you perceive the gastness of her eye?
> Nay, if you stare, we shall hear more anon.
> Behold her well; I pray you, look upon her.
> Do you see, gentlemen? Nay, guiltiness
> Will speak, though tongues were out of use. *(lines 105–10)*

The way Bianca had entered, expressing concern for Cassio, is now patterned by Emilia's arrival, 'What's the matter, husband?' Her allegiance informs her words and her attitude here. She echoes her husband in calling Bianca a 'strumpet', and though in reply Bianca speaks for all three women, her cry goes unheard:

> I am no strumpet, but of life as honest
> As you that thus abuse me. *(lines 122–3)*

Emilia has left Desdemona to come and tend her husband and, in supporting him, she turns upon Bianca, who as another woman should be a natural ally. At this very moment, elsewhere Desdemona is trying in vain to plead her innocence as her husband denounces her as a 'strumpet'.

The scene ends with Iago directing Emilia to go and tell Othello what has happened. It is the last time that Bianca is seen in the play. Her fate is uncertain but the text perhaps implies that Iago is taking her into custody, 'Come, mistress, you must tell's another tale'. His final words, addressed to the audience, acknowledge how events are moving to a climax:

> This is the night
> That either makes me, or fordoes me quite.   *(lines 128–9)*

Act 5 Scene 2

The original stage directions indicate that Othello enters with a light and Desdemona is 'in her bed'. Othello's speech functions as a soliloquy but Desdemona's presence makes the sequence tense. Othello is calm and controlled, believing in the justice and honour of 'the cause', which make it both necessary and right that 'she must die'. The light becomes a metaphor for her life, and his words offer a degree of detachment within which he is clear about the moral imperative to act against the 'cunning'st pattern of excelling nature'. However, when he bends to kiss her, his emotions threaten to interfere with his role as a minister of justice:

> O balmy breath, that dost almost persuade
> Justice to break her sword!   *(lines 16–17)*

The experience prompts an agony of antithetical impulses expressed in 'cruel tears', 'this sorrow's heavenly' and 'It strikes where it doth love.'

When Desdemona wakes, Othello is initially calm, encouraging her to pray to cleanse her soul:

> I would not kill thy unpreparèd spirit;
> No – heaven forfend! – I would not kill thy soul.   *(lines 31–2)*

As she questions Othello's reasons for his passion, he accuses her of giving the handkerchief to Cassio. Although she denies it, he assumes she is lying and calls her a 'perjured woman'. She urges him to send for Cassio, and when Othello tells her he is dead (as he presumes) her response, 'Alas, he is betrayed, and I undone', angers him. Calling her a 'strumpet' and resisting her pleas for some delay, he smothers her, stifling her cries of 'O, Lord, Lord, Lord!'

It is a terrible scene of domestic violence. The dramatic moment is heightened by Emilia's cry, which provides an ironic echo as she calls upon Othello, 'My lord, my lord!' Othello delays attending to Emilia because Desdemona is not quite dead. In contrast to his resonant fluency at the beginning of the scene, his speech is now fragmentary and uncertain as he moves to and from the bed:

> Yes – 'tis Emilia – by and by. – She's dead.
> 'Tis like she comes to speak of Cassio's death:
> The noise was high. Ha! No more moving?
> Still as the grave. Shall she come in? Were't good?
> I think she stirs again. No. What's best to do?
> If she come in, she'll sure speak to my wife –
>
> (Act 5 Scene 2, lines 92-7)

His speculation about Emilia's entrance, which he assumes is to report Cassio's death, prompts his realisation 'I have no wife.' His announcement 'Let me the curtains draw' indicates an important aspect of the original staging which not only explains Emilia's delay in seeing Desdemona but would also have helped the boy actor playing the role of Desdemona. Othello's response to the report of Roderigo's, and not Cassio's, death, 'Then murder's out of tune', cues Desdemona's revival in which she announces that she has been 'falsely murdered'. She affirms her 'guiltless death' and when asked by Emilia, 'O, who hath done this deed?' she absolves Othello. It is difficult to stage Desdemona's revival in modern productions which embrace realism through setting and lighting, but it is important to recognise that Shakespeare's theatre was not naturalistic.

Emilia's defence of Desdemona is clear and forthright. She tells Othello, 'Thou dost belie her', 'she was heavenly true'. What interrupts her fluency is Othello's command, 'Cassio did top her: ask thy husband else.' She can only repeat 'My husband?', which draws from Othello another echo. The word 'husband' is repeated nine times in seventeen lines. Othello cannot understand her shocked response

('What needs this iterance, woman?') and he spells it out, 'I say thy husband. Dost understand the word?' Emilia recognises and acknowledges her own complicity. She has no fear of Othello's threats to her:

> Thou hast not half that power to do me harm
> As I have to be hurt.   *(lines 161–2)*

She describes Desdemona not by name but by the relationship between them, and now 'mistress' takes precedence over 'husband'. When Iago confirms what he told Othello, there is no longer any submission. Emilia throws back Iago's command to 'charm your tongue':

> I will not charm my tongue; I am bound to speak   *(line 183)*

She is 'bound' to her mistress and to truth. Moments earlier she had accurately defined Othello with words more habitually attached to Iago. Her challenge to her husband had been to 'Disprove this villain' as she pointed to Othello. She vigorously declares:

> Villainy, villainy, villainy!
> I think upon't, I think – I smell't – O villainy!
> . . .
> O villainy, villainy!   *(lines 189–92)*

The repetitions of 'husband' have now been overlaid with the judgement 'villainy'. Iago and Othello are for the moment yoked, and Emilia takes control.

Her husband commands her, 'I charge you get you home', but Emilia has no hesitation in refusing to defer to him. She is clear about the moral imperative:

> 'Tis proper I obey him, but not now.
> Perchance, Iago, I will ne'er go home.   *(lines 195–6)*

Because of his faith in Iago, Othello remains convinced of Desdemona's infidelity and he tells Gratiano that 'she was foul'. Gratiano reveals that Brabantio has died and Shakespeare provides a sympathetic insight into the tragedy of a father dying of grief at the loss of his daughter.

As Othello reveals more of the details of the plotting and mentions the handkerchief, Emilia insists on speaking out. Although her husband tells her 'Be wise and get you home', her refusal is immediate and succinct, 'I will not.' She confesses giving Iago the handkerchief and, ignoring Iago's interjections ('Villainous whore!' and 'Filth, thou liest!'), she reveals the truth. Her conclusion about Othello's marriage patently applies to her own situation too:

> . . . what should such a fool
> Do with so good a wife?   *(lines 231–2)*

A flurry of activity then erupts in which Othello stabs Iago and is then disarmed by Montano. Iago stabs Emilia before exiting. The lines which follow the action point the parallels between the two couples:

GRATIANO   The woman falls; sure he hath killed his wife.

. . .

GRATIANO   He's gone, but his wife's killed.
MONTANO   'Tis a notorious villain.   *(lines 234, 235–6)*

Montano takes control and will pursue Iago, but first he orders Gratiano to guard the door to restrain Othello. Emilia's dying words speak of the relationship that now takes precedence for her: 'O, lay me by my mistress' side.' Emilia replicates poor Barbary. She asks 'What did thy song bode, lady?' and her sympathetic understanding is reflected in the way she echoes 'Willow, willow, willow.'

Othello has 'another weapon' in his chamber but calls to Gratiano, claiming he is unarmed and only wishes to speak to him. When Gratiano enters, Othello confronts him, 'Behold, I have a weapon', and invokes the image of Othello the soldier, who in the past had dealt with 'more impediments' than twenty times the resistance that Gratiano presents. But Othello then dismisses his impulse to flee as a 'vain boast' and reassures Gratiano that 'Here is my journey's end' as he turns to the bed. His speech climaxes in an agony of grief: 'O Desdemon! Dead Desdemon! Dead! O! O!'

Lodovico now takes charge and, in his defence, Othello describes himself as an 'honourable murderer' and asserts, 'For naught did I in hate, but all in honour.' With the bodies of Desdemona and Emilia lying on stage, Cassio pleads his innocence in words which take us back to the scene's solemn opening, 'Dear general, I never gave you cause.' Othello not only accepts his statement but indeed asks Cassio's forgiveness: 'I ask your pardon'. He can see Iago now for the 'demi-devil' he is, and his expression of this perception silences Iago:

> Demand me nothing; what you know, you know.
> From this time forth I never will speak word. *(lines 300–1)*

Iago's role is complete; there is no point in speculation. Indeed his own words, 'what you know, you know', warn against attempts to find a consistency or coherent motivation in his actions. All the machinations of the plot are unravelled by reference to letters, 'another discontented paper' and the reported confession of Roderigo. Lodovico affirms that 'Cassio rules in Cyprus' and arrests Othello.

But Othello seizes control away from Lodovico with a peremptory 'Soft you; a word or two'. He moves swiftly from the concise reminder of his service to the state with 'No more of that.' He has now recognised that his public role is ultimately irrelevant. It is his integrity as an individual which must be restored and the focus shifts to the private man. His self-judgement, 'one that loved not wisely, but too well', has been much misunderstood. It is not that he believes that love should be restrained, ordered, or calculated to please the prevailing social attitude. It is the intensity of his love that made him vulnerable. His words have a studied control; the verse is firm, resonant and purposeful with surging enjambement (see page 80). He is offering a distillation of experience from which others might benefit ('Set you down this') before taking his own life.

Death is a reconciliation for Othello and Desdemona. He had said to Iago:

> I'd have thee live,
> For in my sense 'tis happiness to die. *(lines 286–7)*

He dies in an act of love:

> I kissed thee ere I killed thee: no way but this,
> Killing myself, to die upon a kiss. *(lines 354–5)*

The kiss seals their union. Othello's suicide pre-empts trial, verdict and sentence, enabling the dramatist to move rapidly to a conclusion with the conventional tableau of the 'tragic loading of this bed'. Cassio, now Lord Governor of the isle, is given charge of Iago with licence to decide the 'censure of this hellish villain: / The time, the place, the torture', whilst Lodovico departs to relate events to those in Venice. Significantly, in view of the priorities just expressed by Othello's words and actions, Lodovico will tell the story with 'heavy heart'.

Act 5: Critical review

Act 5 (like Act 1) takes place at night. Darkness facilitates Iago's plotting against both Cassio and Roderigo. The latter is frequently dismissed as foolish and unimportant but Iago recognises the threat he poses. Roderigo and Cassio must die. Iago projects responsibility for the attack upon Cassio onto Bianca. Her genuine concern is presented by Iago as evidence of women's ability to dissemble. The action of the final two scenes overlaps as what is generally known as the play's 'double time' scheme contributes to the intensity of its conclusion. At the same time as Bianca is asserting 'I am no strumpet', Desdemona is pleading her innocence, but neither woman is believed. Emilia's entrance in Act 5 Scene 2 marks the point at which the two strands merge into a single linear narrative.

The rivalry that had figured so strongly in the play's opening is recalled in the final opposition of Cassio and Iago. Events bring about a double reversal of fortune. Cassio had lost and Iago had gained the position of lieutenant but, ultimately, Cassio will rule in Cyprus with Iago at his mercy. Iago's earlier enigmatic 'I am not what I am' is now patterned in the wilful and unhelpful impenetrability of 'what you know, you know'. The play also charts the waste of constant, loving women, underestimated and abused by the men they love. The real tragedy for Desdemona, Emilia and Bianca is the way their marital and emotional bonding takes precedence over their common cause.

In the last act, Othello transcends uncertainty and perplexity in an affirmation of the primacy of the 'heart'. It was his 'hand' which 'threw a pearl away'. Emotional intensity triumphs. Gratiano's 'All that's spoke is marred!' offers commentary upon the ways in which language has been used to conceal duplicity and create perplexity. Ultimately, Othello sees clearly and acts decisively, recognising that what matters above all is the truth of emotion. The epitaph that Cassio provides for Othello is concise and sensitive: 'For he was great of heart.' The phrase resonates powerfully. Perhaps too many academic critics closeted in their studies have undervalued the theatrical and emotional impact of the tragedy. Lodovico will return to Venice and will retell the story of 'This heavy act with heavy heart'.

From the stuff of somewhat crude and melodramatic prose fiction, Shakespeare created a play that has the intensity and excitement of happening for the first time whenever it is performed. As events unfold, an audience is drawn into the world of the play and is held by the moment-by-moment intensity of the experience. The stage history of *Othello* is punctuated by accounts of members of an audience intervening in the forlorn hope of halting the plunge to catastrophe. The dramatic experience denies any passive complacency in response to the events. This section seeks to explore how such a remarkable play was crafted. Shakespeare not only reflects the concerns and attitudes of his time but also vigorously challenges conventional thinking. His decision to make a black man a tragic hero was astonishing and this choice as well as the play's exploration of relationships can be illuminated by reference to his other work.

The tight focus of *Othello*, its relatively small cast and its searing exploration of sexual jealousy have earned it the label of 'domestic tragedy'. However, this is not to belittle the play, nor to imply that it lacks a political dimension. Setting the play in Venice, within the context of the threat of a Turkish invasion of Cyprus, ensures that considerations of national identity are embraced. Shakespeare provides a broader canvas for the play's intense focus upon the plight of the individual struggling to hold onto a sense of self under siege.

What did Shakespeare write?

It is sobering to realise that there does not exist a single, authoritative text of any of Shakespeare's plays. He wrote scripts, not books, and more than half his plays were not printed during his lifetime. The first collected edition of his plays was published in 1623, seven years after his death, and for plays like *Antony and Cleopatra*, *Macbeth*, *As You Like It*, *Twelfth Night* and *The Tempest* this is as near to what Shakespeare actually wrote as anyone can get. No manuscripts of his plays have survived and, where there are rival early editions, establishing a text is a matter which has absorbed scholars for centuries.

Some of Shakespeare's plays were published during his lifetime in quarto format (comparable to modern paperbacks) and these texts differ from the versions printed in the later Folio. *Othello* was first printed in 1622 in quarto format. In the Folio which appeared the following year, it is the ninth play in the Tragedies' section. It is one of only seven plays which include a list of *dramatis personae* at the end of the text. It would seem that each of these lists is designed to fill up what would otherwise be blank paper. The list for *Othello* includes some descriptive additions: 'the Moor' and 'father to Desdemona'. There are also phrases which define the characters. Iago is described as 'a villain' and Roderigo as 'a gulled gentleman', but it would seem that this text derives from the printing house and it cannot be taken as having authorial authority. The version of the play which appears in the First Folio is significantly different from the text that was published the year before. It contains about 160 more lines than the Quarto. Desdemona's willow song only appears in the Folio text and Emilia's role in the later stages of the play is developed. There are over a thousand differences between the two texts. For example, over 50 oaths appear only in the Quarto text. Scholars believe that the two texts are based upon different versions of the play and that the existence of both texts provides an opportunity to reflect upon Shakespeare's creative process of rewriting and revision.

Modern editors draw on both texts but the result is that they each produce as it were a 'third' version of the text. This Guide follows the New Cambridge edition of the play (also used in Cambridge School Shakespeare). Its editor, Norman Sanders, acknowledges that the text which he has produced conflates Q and F but, interestingly and importantly, he argues that the text then in some ways becomes, like a performance of the play, an interpretation in itself. It is vitally important in studying the play to recognise what might be referred to as the instability of the text. It helps to explain why actors and critics offer different interpretations. There can be no definitive text of *Othello*. The existence of variants is evidence that Shakespeare was working within a collaborative medium. The reality of live performance, and the pressures upon such a creative process, almost invariably result in a more fluid and less stable text. Editors must intervene in preparing a text and inevitably such a process shapes the reader's response to the text.

The division of Shakespeare's plays into acts and scenes is essentially editorial rather than authorial, and the scheme dates back essentially to 1623, when Heminge and Condell produced the First

Folio edition of Shakespeare's plays. The convention for scene division that they chose to adopt was that a new scene is marked once the action has been punctuated by the stage having been cleared of actors. Though the first editors occasionally nodded (the Queen is left on stage between Acts 3 and 4 of *Hamlet*), the convention is generally observed and it just happens to be a different convention from, say, French Classical Theatre, where the entrance of a new character requires a new scene. The convention has nothing to do with changing the scenery and comparatively little to do with an audience's experience in the theatre. The action may be disjointed or it may be flexible and fluid. The audience's experience in the theatre is determined much more by the pace of the verse and the requirements of exits and entrances.

There is also the matter of stage directions. Shakespeare's preferred method is to integrate indications for action in the dialogue: when Desdemona is demonstrating to Iago her commitment to Othello she states, 'Here I kneel' (Act 4 Scene 2, line 150); the cue for the Musicians is given by Cassio, 'Masters, play here' (Act 3 Scene 1, line 1); and Othello's deference to the authority of Venice is indicated when he takes the letter from Lodovico, 'I kiss the instrument of their pleasures' (Act 4 Scene 1, line 207). In this way, Shakespeare constructs the stage picture and creates moments of tableau like the 'tragic loading of this bed' (Act 5 Scene 2, line 359). The process of reading any play must engage with the indications for staging, and modern editors seek to assist readers by adding directions to their texts. In most cases, matters such as the insertion of entrances and exits merely involve an uncontroversial tidying up of the text, but there are occasions when an editor's indication of what happens on stage becomes interpretative (see page 30).

What did Shakespeare read?

The business of disentangling strands of influence and understanding the process of adaptation can be complex and confusing where there are several possible sources for a particular play. However, in the case of *Othello* it seems that Shakespeare worked from just one source: *The story of Disdemona of Venice and the Moorish Captain*, by Giraldi Cinthio, published in his collection, *Hecatommithi* (1565). Shakespeare modifies, expands and invents material to shape what is essentially a narrative into dramatic form. The only character whom

Cinthio names is the heroine and what follows is a summary of his
story:

> The Moor of Venice was a brave military figure and
> Disdemona fell in love with him because of his work. There
> was some opposition from her family but they married and
> lived happily in Venice with no conflict or unhappiness. The
> Moor was appointed to take a group of soldiers to the
> garrisoned Cyprus. He felt honoured but concerned about
> what he saw as an impossible choice. Either he would have to
> subject his wife to the risk of the long voyage or he would
> have to leave her behind in Venice. Disdemona was clear about
> her desire to accompany him and share any dangers with him.
> They had a completely calm journey.
>
> In the Company was an Ensign, who was good-looking but
> depraved. The Moor had no idea of the man's true nature but
> judged him to be a courageous and reliable soldier. His wife
> had also accompanied him to Cyprus and she and Disdemona
> were good friends. There was also a Captain who spent a lot of
> time with the Moor and his wife. Disdemona knew how much
> her husband liked him, so she was always kind to the Captain,
> which pleased her husband.
>
> The wicked Ensign fell in love with Disdemona and he sought
> to find a way to enjoy her. He feared for his life if the Moor
> found out. He tried all sorts of approaches but Disdemona did
> not respond at all. He thought she preferred the Captain and,
> therefore, he wished to remove the Captain but his love for
> Disdemona also turned to hatred. If he could not enjoy her, he
> did not want anyone else to have her. His plan was to tell the
> Moor of his wife's adultery with the Captain but he knew that
> he would have to wait for the right moment.
>
> Later, when on guard, the Captain wounded a soldier and, as a
> result, he was dismissed by the Moor. Disdemona was upset
> and sought to intercede on the Captain's behalf. The Moor told
> the Ensign about his wife's persistence and this gave the
> Ensign the idea of making the Moor suspicious of her
> motives.The Moor became melancholy and Disdemona

pursued the Captain's case, particularly as the Captain and the soldier he had injured had become reconciled. The Moor became angry with her, she became frightened and promised to say no more.

He returned to the Ensign, pleading with him to tell him what he knew. Reluctantly, the Ensign told the Moor that the reason Disdemona was supporting the Captain was because she was 'taking her pleasure' with him when he visited their house. He suggested that Disdemona had become disgusted with Othello's colour. Although the Moor believed the Ensign's account, he aggressively challenged him, prompting the Ensign's defence of love and his claim that the Captain had confided in him.The Moor insisted that he wanted to see evidence of his wife's infidelity, which he was told would be difficult to provide now that he had banished the Captain from his house.

The Ensign was aware that Disdemona's chastity made providing proof of her infidelity difficult. He decided to steal her precious handkerchief when she paid one of her regular visits to see his wife and play with their three-year-old daughter. Using the child to distract Disdemona, the Ensign took the handkerchief from Disdemona's girdle. Discovering its loss a few days later, Disdemona was frightened that the Moor would ask her for it.

The Ensign put it in the Captain's bed, who went to return it at a time when he knew the Moor would be away. By chance, the Moor returned home to see the departing Captain. Furiously, the Moor questioned Disdemona about who had been knocking at the door but, truthfully, she said she did not know. The Moor confided in the Ensign, who arranged for the Moor to watch him in conversation with the Captain, during which the Captain appeared excited and demonstrative. Subsequently, the Ensign told the Moor that the Captain had been telling him about his regular assignations with Disdemona, at the last of which she had given him her handkerchief.

Believing that the handkerchief was the crucial piece of evidence, the Moor asked his wife for it. Frightened, she blushed as she pretended to look for it. He left her, determined to find a way to bring about the deaths of his wife and the Captain without any suspicion of his involvement. He became self-absorbed and Disdemona expressed concern to him and, in distress, pleaded with the Ensign's wife for any insight her husband might have about the reason for the Moor's melancholy.

The Ensign's wife knew about her husband's involvement in the plot against Disdemona but she was too frightened of him to say anything to Disdemona. She merely advised her to be loving to her husband.

In response to the Moor's insistence that he see the hand-kerchief, the Ensign arranged for the Moor to see a woman at the Captain's lodging making herself a copy of it. Totally convinced of his wife's infidelity, the Moor and the Ensign planned murder. The Ensign was reluctant to kill the Captain but he was persuaded by entreaty and money to mount an attack when the Captain left a brothel. However, the Captain's vigour and loud cries foiled the plan and the Ensign was only able to wound him in the thigh. Confident, though, that the wound would prove fatal, the Ensign used the cover of dark-ness to create the impression that he arrived to offer assistance.

When Disdemona heard of the attack she was distressed, which further confirmed her guilt to her husband. He and the Ensign devised a plan to beat her to death with a stocking full of sand (so that there would be no marks upon her body) and then cause the roof to collapse upon her so that it would look like an accident. The Moor hid the Ensign in a closet, and when Disdemona went to investigate a noise the Ensign attacked her, while the Moor harangued her for her infidelity. She appealed for divine justice. The plan worked and there was widespread grief at the terrible accident.

Disdemona's appeal to God was answered by the Moor's grief and madness as he searched for his wife. He developed an implacable hatred for the Ensign. He dismissed him from the company and would have killed him but feared retribution from the authorities. As a result, the Ensign vowed revenge upon the Moor.

He forged an alliance with the Captain, promising to help discover the assailant who had injured him so severely that he now had a wooden leg. On their return to Venice, he told the Captain that the Moor, believing in his wife's infidelity with the Captain, had attacked him before murdering Disdemona. The Captain laid charges in the Venetian court against the Moor, with the Ensign as his witness. The Moor was arrested in Cyprus, brought back to Venice and tortured to make him confess. Courageously, he denied everything. He was imprisoned, then exiled but, ultimately, he was killed by Disdemona's relatives, which was judged to be an appropriate outcome.

The Ensign returned to his own country and, as a result of a plot against one of his companions being thwarted, he was put on the rack. His injuries were so severe that he later died.

God was judged to have revenged the murder of the innocent Disdemona. The whole story was subsequently related by the Ensign's wife after her husband's death.

Cinthio tells his story in far more leisurely fashion than does Shakespeare. The action spreads over months and extends beyond Disdemona's death. Roderigo is Shakespeare's invention. He provides a foil for Iago and might initially tempt an audience to sympathise with what seems a legitimate grievance. However, he is soon material for Iago's skilful exploitation and abuse. By his love for Desdemona, Roderigo provides evidence of 'the wealthy, curlèd darlings of our nation' whom she has rejected. Like many of the characters in the play, he is rendered vulnerable by his love. In Cinthio's story, there is no storm and the Moor and Disdemona travel and arrive safely together. The Captain (Cassio) has had no part in the development of the relationship between the Moor and Disdemona and the loss of his job has nothing to do with the Ensign. There is no suggestion that the Iago figure is motivated by being passed over for promotion. His love for Disdemona turns to hatred and he develops an intense jealousy of the Captain. Her death is contrived to appear accidental and the actual details seem absurd. Shakespeare takes the decision to invest Othello with the qualities of an 'honourable murderer'. The Venetians deport and try the Moor. Despite torture he does not recount what happened and so escapes death. After imprisonment, followed by banishment, he is killed by Disdemona's relatives and Cinthio adds 'as he deserved to be'. Sometime later, the Ensign is tortured about another matter and, although he reveals nothing, he dies 'miserably' as a result of his injuries. In Shakespeare's play, Othello is open and honest about his actions and the reasons for them. He takes his own life in an act of judicial execution and all references to torture are applied exclusively to Iago. He declares 'I never will speak word' to which Gratiano replies:

> Torments will ope your lips.   *(Act 5 Scene 2, line 303)*

and the threat is confirmed in the closing moments of the play as Lodovico urges Cassio '. . . the torture, O, enforce it!'

In Cinthio's story, the women are more shadowy figures than in Shakespeare's play. However, certain details from the source seem to have shaped both theatrical practice and critical response to the play, sometimes blurring the effect of the changes Shakespeare has made in characterisation. There are examples of editors assuming that Shakespeare has followed Cinthio more closely than is in fact the case.

Shakespeare's decision to have Desdemona marry Othello against determined parental opposition makes her stronger than her counterpart. In the senate scene, she speaks fluently and assuredly of the totality of her commitment to her husband. Emilia is employed not by her but by Othello, for he instructs Iago, 'I prithee, let thy wife attend on her'. When we first see the women together on their arrival in Cyprus, there is little sense of any relationship between them beyond that of mistress and maid. In the original, the Ensign's wife and Disdemona were great friends. The Ensign's wife is a confidante and she knows about her own husband's duplicity, but dare not speak for fear of him. There is no such relationship between the women in Shakespeare's play. He establishes clearly the way in which each woman's marital bond takes priority over any female friendship.

Bianca fulfils the role of two quite different women in Shakespeare's source. One of the women at the Captain's (Cassio's) lodging is skilled in embroidery and he asks her to copy the handkerchief. She is distinct from the prostitute whose house he leaves before being set upon by the Ensign. Shakespeare invests much more in the character of Bianca than is required by these two narrative strands. Although she is described in the Folio list of characters as 'a courtesan', this designation is unlikely to be authorial and the play merely gives us allegations rather than evidence of her promiscuity.

Cinthio's account ends by asserting that events showed how God revenged 'the innocence of Disdemona' but the role of the Ensign's wife is important in unravelling details. It was she 'who had all along known the truth'. From this hint perhaps, Shakespeare developed Emilia's remarkable authority in the final scene.

Tragedy

In a modern play by Willy Russell, *Educating Rita*, Frank explains to a sceptical Rita why a report in the paper, 'Man Killed by Falling Tree', is not a tragedy. It may be tragic but tragedy 'is inevitable'. His definition is broadly based upon Aristotle. The classical notion of tragedy is that it charts the fall of a great man from a position of high esteem and power to his death. Of crucial importance is the notion that the protagonist has a fault, or flaw, in his character which brings about his downfall. The experience of tragedy excites in the members of the audience intense emotions of pity and fear as they share in the experience of the central characters and undergo a purgation, or catharsis. Participating in the process prompts feelings of exhaustion, cleansing and enrichment.

However it can be unhelpful to assume that Shakespeare shaped his plays within this mould. Perhaps there is no such thing as 'Shakespearean tragedy' but, more straightforwardly, tragedies by Shakespeare. Certainly, Shakespeare does not observe strict rules of genre, though aspects of Aristotle's pattern can be seen to apply to *Othello*. In one of his own plays (*Antigone*) the French playwright, Jean Anouilh, offered a description of tragedy which has particular force for *Othello*:

> The spring is wound up tight. It will uncoil of itself. That's what's so convenient about tragedy.
>
> It only needs the slightest turn of the wrist to set it going. Or a glance at a girl lifting her arms in the street, or when you wake on a fine morning a yearning to be respected, or perhaps in an evening one question too many. Anything. And then it's enough, there's nothing else to be done. The rest is automatic. It's precise, accurate, oiled since the beginning of time. Death,

treason, sorrow are there ready, along with the outbursts, thunderings and silences. Above all, the silences. The silence when the executioner's axe is raised in the final scene; the silence in the opening moments when the two lovers stand, naked, face to face for the first time in the darkened room, not daring to move. The silence when the acclaim of the crowd resounds around the victor – and you think of a film without any sound, with the mouths gaping and silent, all the noise is no more than a picture, and the victor, already defeated, is alone in the midst of his silence.

Tragedy is clean; restful and certain. It's got nothing to do with melodrama, with wicked villains, persecuted innocents, avengers and last-minute repentance. In melodrama, death is accidental and horrifying. You might perhaps be saved, saved perhaps by the fine young man who's gone for the police. In tragedy, all is calm. In the first place, we're among ourselves – he who kills is as innocent as he who gets killed – it all depends on what part you are playing.

And then, above all, tragedy is restful. You know there's no hope, no vain, illusory hope. You're trapped. The sky has fallen on you and there's nothing to do but shout – not groan, no, not complain – shout out in a loud voice all those things that you never thought you'd be able to say, never knew you had it in you to say. But not because it will do you any good, you say them for their own sake, you say them because you learn a lot.

In melodrama, you argue because you hope to escape. That's vulgar; it's practical. In tragedy, argument is a luxury enjoyed by kings. There's no longer any escape.

Anouilh's metaphor of the spring captures the unremitting nature of the action of *Othello*. There is an inexorable mechanism at work: events have to run their course. His distinction between melodrama and tragedy is valuable. In the latter, an audience is implicated in the action for 'we're among ourselves'. We are encouraged to go beyond simple black-and-white oppositions. Indeed, immediate identification of hero and villain may not be easy. Much more can be mined from

Anouilh's description of tragedy. His statement that 'all is calm' might well be the basis of analysing how Act 5 of Shakespeare's play works.

What was Shakespeare's England like?

Politics

Defining *Othello* as a 'domestic' tragedy has carried with it a value judgement. The hero is not a king, like Macbeth or Lear, and therefore his tragedy is frequently thought to have no significant political consequences or implications beyond the scope of personal relationships. However, the location of the action is important. At the time Shakespeare was writing, plays with an Italian setting were popular. Venice, a thriving commercial centre, had two different characteristics. It was seen as a place of romance, with cultural values and yet also, as the birthplace of Niccolò Machiavelli (1469–1527), it was associated with poisonings and vice. The action of the play soon shifts to an island under threat of invasion.

The Turks had attacked Cyprus in 1570 and had conquered it in the following year. Cyprus was a Venetian protectorate and the conflict between Venice and Turkey was between Christians and infidels: the historical background provides a context for the narrative. Virginia Mason Vaughan argues that 'Othello's loss . . . does have frightening consequences for Venice, a city precariously balanced on the frontiers of Christian civilisation'. The opening chapter of her book '*Othello': A Contextual History* sets out an important case for acknowledging the particular implications of the play's setting.

> In contrast to Othello, Venice seems sure of its identity as the play begins – urbane and civilised; as Brabantio exclaims, 'This is Venice; / My house is not a grange' (1.1.106–7). Centuries of legal and governmental tradition have defined Venice as the locus of rational judgment . . . Caught in a liminal zone between Venice's Christian civility and the Ottomite's pagan barbarism is Cyprus, a Venetian colony under siege. Cyprus is the frontier, the uttermost edge of western civilisation, simultaneously vulnerable to attack from without and subversion from within . . . Cyprus's geographical and political position mirror Othello's psychic situation. Like Cyprus, Othello can be colonised by Venice – he can be put to

use. But he can never become wholly Venetian. This liminal
positioning makes him vulnerable to Iago's wiles and, like
Cyprus, if he is not fortified, he will 'turn Turk'.

She claims that the opposition of Venetian and Turk continues
through the play, culminating in Othello's final speech in which he
ultimately conquers the threat presented by 'a turbaned Turk'. In her
reading, 'the precariousness of a nation's identity – not just an
individual's – lurks behind the tragedy of Othello and his wife'.

Race and colour

In medieval England, and throughout European folk-lore, the colour
black was associated with the demonic. By extension, it came to
embrace not only ideas of sin and death but the negative connotations
of defilement and all the opposite characterisation of 'white'. Eliza-
bethans were fascinated by travellers' tales and the accounts offered
there of the appearance, behaviour, manners, customs (including canni-
balism) and social interaction of groups of people unlike themselves.
Such narratives often suggested that natives went about naked and this
became associated with savagery, depravity and a predatory sexuality.

There is evidence that there were a considerable number of black
people in England in the late sixteenth century. Elizabeth I gave
licence for a sea captain to transport all 'Negroes and Blackamoors'
from England in 1601. It would seem that they had arrived in England
as a result of the conflicts with Spain and were slaves or servants.
When Shakespeare was writing *Othello*, therefore, his audience's
awareness of blackamoors would be as men who were slaves or
servants, not people with status or authority in society.

Drama of the period makes a good deal of use of black characters.
Playwrights were drawn to the potential offered by the attraction of the
'other', the visual contrast the character provides and the scope to
explore unusual aspects of character and behaviour. Generally, the
black roles before Othello confirmed the assumptions that such
characters were morally deficient, sexually active and attracted to
white women. Before writing *Othello*, Shakespeare had included black
characters in two earlier plays, Aaron in *Titus Andronicus* and the
Prince of Morocco in *The Merchant of Venice*.

Although *Titus Andronicus* is one of Shakespeare's earliest plays,
there is an increasing respect for its qualities. Aaron is an evil

character. He has an adulterous relationship with Tamora, the defeated Queen of the Goths who becomes Empress of Rome. Aaron identifies himself as sexually voracious, relishing the opportunity 'to wanton with this queen'. He also sees himself as a figure of revenge:

> Vengeance is in my heart, death in my hand,
> Blood and revenge are hammering in my head.
>
> *(Act 2 Scene 3, lines 38–9)*

But Shakespeare complicates an audience's evaluation by giving Aaron a parental role. Tamora gives birth to a son, whose black skin reveals that the father is Aaron and not her husband. She sends the baby to Aaron for him to destroy, but he will not do so. Cradling his son, he offers commentary upon the shared bond of their colour:

> Coal-black is better than another hue
> In that it scorns to bear another hue.
>
> *(Act 4 Scene 2, lines 99–100)*

He is fiercely protective of the child and is determined to care for him:

> Come on, you thick-lipped slave, I'll bear you hence,
> For it is you that puts us to our shifts.
> I'll make you feed on berries and on roots,
> And fat on curds and whey, and suck the goat,
> And cabin in a cave, and bring you up
> To be a warrior and command a camp.
>
> *(Act 4 Scene 2, lines 176–81)*

When he is arrested, he promises a full confession of his crimes if his son is saved. His uncompromising commitment to evil is tempered by an extraordinary tenderness and love, regardless of the fact that the child's cries reveal his whereabouts to those pursuing him. Aaron is judged by the Romans to be 'an inhuman dog' but the role suggests Shakespeare's early awareness of the theatrical, even tragic, potential of a Moor.

In *The Merchant of Venice*, the Prince of Morocco is the first of Portia's suitors to elect to take the casket test to try to win her hand in marriage. Like Aaron, he conforms to the stereotype of the black man attracted to a white woman but, once again, Shakespeare complicates an audience's judgement. Although in performance he is too often presented as an exaggerated figure who prompts laughter, there is a dignity in his consciousness of 'otherness'. In his first line he appeals against what he recognises will be an immediate judgement based upon his colour:

> Mislike me not for my complexion,
> The shadowed livery of the burnished sun,
> To whom I am a neighbour and near bred.
>
> *(Act 2 Scene 1, lines 1–3)*

His boastfulness about his achievements may serve perhaps, like Othello's, to mask an uncertainty, even a vulnerability:

> By this scimitar,
> That slew the Sophy and a Persian prince
> That won three fields of Sultan Solyman,
> I would o'er-stare the sternest eyes that look,
> Outbrave the heart most daring on the earth,
> Pluck the young sucking cubs from the she-bear,
> Yea, mock the lion when a roars for prey,
> To win thee, lady. *(Act 2 Scene 1, lines 24–31)*

Shakespeare gives him more time in the play than his somewhat contemptible successor, the Prince of Aragon. Morocco leaves the stage hoping for 'good fortune', which he acknowledges will determine his fate to be 'blest – or cursed'st among men!'. It is not until six scenes later that he makes choice of the caskets. Portia describes him as 'this noble prince' and although he will fail the casket test, his 48-line speech of reflection commands an audience's attention and respect. His reasons for choosing the gold casket cannot be despised and he accepts his fate with dignity. It is to his credit that he makes no demands upon Portia once his fate is decided. He leaves immediately because his emotional investment in the enterprise has been sincere: 'I have too grieved a heart / To take a tedious leave'.

The characters of Aaron and Morocco show that, even fairly early in his career, Shakespeare was not only aware of the dramatic possibilities of black characters but also conscious of ways in which the established stereotype might be challenged. Nevertheless, his decision to craft a tragedy with a black man as the protagonist was a remarkable decision. Shakespeare wrote his plays in an England which was committed to its own sense of itself, its culture and its values. Social cohesion can be reinforced by projecting fears and frustrations upon an 'out-group' and it is all too easy to vilify a tiny minority. The conventional, unthinking attitudes of Jacobean times might from a modern perspective be labelled 'racist', but there is a continuing debate about where Shakespeare stood. Some critics feel that the character of Othello confirms the cultural prejudices of the time, while others argue that the play as a whole challenges such easy assumptions. There is agreement that the text contains the stereotype of the black man, but critics disagree in their judgements of how Shakespeare uses such a stereotype.

Two critics writing in 1987 illustrate the different points of view. Anthony Barthelemy claims:

> However successful Shakespeare's manipulation of the stereotype may be, Othello remains identifiable as a version of that type . . . Shakespeare's black Moor never possesses the power or desire to subvert civic and natural order.

On the other hand, Karen Newman's view is:

> Shakespeare was certainly subject to the racist, sexist, and colonist discourses of his time, but by making the black Othello a hero, and by making Desdemona's love for Othello, and her transgression of her society's norms for women in choosing him, sympathetic, Shakespeare's play stands in a contestatory relationship to the hegemonic ideologies of race and gender in early modern England.

Marriage

Generalisation is always dangerous. It is often asserted that the concept of marriage during the Elizabethan/Jacobean period was very different from nowadays, but attitudes were shifting and conventional assumptions were being questioned. Although pamphlets and sermons from the pulpit promoted the appropriateness of silent, obedient and malleable women, in the theatre patriarchal attitudes were under scrutiny.

Shakespeare gives us many forceful, fluent female characters. Encouragement to make judgements of their social behaviour is provided within the plays themselves. At the end of *The Taming of the Shrew*, Katherine is invited by her husband to tell the 'headstrong women', Bianca and the Widow, 'What duty they do owe their lords and husbands'. Katherine's response reminds women that 'they are bound to serve, love and obey', echoing the words of the wedding ceremony from *The Book of Common Prayer* (1552), 'Wylte thou obey him, and serue him, love, honor, and kepe him, in sickenes and in health?' But Katherine makes it clear that she regards the duty a woman 'owes to her husband' as one that must be qualified. She must be obedient to his 'honest will'. She has come to recognise from the experience she has gained throughout her own journey during the course of the play that what matters most is an understanding that goes beyond words and sympathy. Shakespeare's priority in reflecting upon the aspirations of so many couples in his plays is to promote the merit of partnership and mutual respect. He offers a compelling definition of love in *Sonnet 116*:

> Let me not to the marriage of true minds
> Admit impediments; love is not love
> Which alters when it alteration finds,
> Or bends with the remover to remove.
> O no, it is an ever-fixèd mark
> That looks on tempests and is never shaken;
> It is the star to every wand'ring bark,
> Whose worth's unknown, although his height be taken.
> Love's not Time's fool, though rosy lips and cheeks
> Within his bending sickle's compass come;
> Love alters not with his brief hours and weeks,
> But bears it out even to the edge of doom.
>   If this be error and upon me proved,
>   I never writ, nor no man ever loved.

In *Othello*, obedience is a central concern. There are 11 references to 'obey' and 'obedience' in the text. Through the figure of Desdemona, Shakespeare also explores (and endorses, as he does in *A*

Midsummer Night's Dream, *Romeo and Juliet* and *Cymbeline*) a daughter's right to choose her own husband. Brabantio has respected Desdemona's decision to reject Roderigo's proposal of marriage ('my daughter is not for thee') but after her elopement with Othello, Brabantio seeks to exert a patriarchal control:

> Come hither, gentle mistress;
> Do you perceive in all this noble company
> Where most you owe obedience?   *(Act 1 Scene 3, lines 176–8)*

In Desdemona's reply, Shakespeare presents a courteous, yet confident assertion of the need for fathers to acknowledge and respect a daughter's maturity. A father's authority is inevitably, and appropriately, replaced by that of a husband:

> My noble father,
> I do perceive here a divided duty:
> To you I am bound for life and education;
> My life and education both do learn me
> How to respect you. You are lord of all my duty;
> I am hitherto your daughter. But here's my husband;
> And so much duty as my mother showed
> To you, preferring you before her father,
> So much I challenge that I may profess
> Due to the Moor my lord.   *(Act 1 Scene 3, lines 178–87)*

Both Desdemona and Emilia give the highest priority to obeying their husbands. Desdemona tells Othello, 'Whate'er you be, I am obedient', and Emilia obeys Iago's instruction not to reveal the whereabouts of the handkerchief. In order to obey her husband, Emilia lies to Desdemona, 'I know not, madam.' However, when Iago's deception is revealed, Emilia is quick to acknowledge her own complicity because of the union of husband and wife. She states clearly that the moral imperative over-rules the marital bond ("Tis proper I obey him, but not now') and she refuses to obey her husband's commands to be silent and to go home. She is, she knows, 'bound' to speak out and she is prepared to declare an independence, 'Perchance, Iago, I will ne'er go home.'

Sexual jealousy

Shakespeare is acutely aware of the dramatic potential of the theme of sexual jealousy. In *Much Ado About Nothing*, Claudio's erroneous suspicions that Hero has been unfaithful to him lead him to reject her at their wedding. The men are united in asserting not only that they are right in their judgement about Hero but also that public exposure of Hero's infidelity is an appropriate action to maintain their male honour. Beatrice exposes such patriarchal tyranny and Shakespeare gives her a powerful voice to challenge conventional attitudes.

Shakespeare writes about sexual jealousy throughout his career, and the character of Claudio is followed not only by Othello but also by Leontes (in *The Winter's Tale*) and Posthumus (in *Cymbeline*). All four husbands wrongly accuse their wives of infidelity. In each play there is a strong, eloquent woman to voice powerful opposition to male complacency. Bound up with the issue of sexual jealousy is the belief that a double standard operates in sexual matters, but Shakespeare is aware how such a notion can be questioned. In one of his very first plays, *The Comedy of Errors*, Adriana uses marital union as an effective argument against licensed male promiscuity. She warns that a husband's infidelity contaminates a wife:

> For if we two be one, and thou play false,
> I do digest the poison of thy flesh,
> Being strumpeted by thy contagion.
> Keep then fair league and truce with thy true bed,
> I live unstained, thou undishonourèd.
>
> *(Act 2 Scene 2, lines 133–7)*

Her words make a powerful case for mutual fidelity as a means of preserving purity and the honour of both husband and wife.

In *Othello*, Emilia takes the issue further. Her analysis of attitudes towards sexual behaviour exposes the illogicality and unfairness of judgements about sexual behaviour which operate differently for men and women:

> Let husbands know
> Their wives have sense like them: they see, and smell,
> And have their palates both for sweet and sour
> As husbands have. What is it that they do

When they change us for others? Is it sport?
I think it is. And doth affection breed it?
I think it doth. Is't frailty that thus errs?
It is so too. And have not we affections,
Desires for sport, and frailty, as men have?

(Act 4 Scene 3, lines 89–97)

Ultimately, Emilia's appeal is for kindness and respect in marriage: 'Then let them use us well'. If they do not and their wives stray then the women are simply following the example set by their husbands: 'their ills instruct us so'.

An awareness that legal and moral codes operated differently at the time Shakespeare was writing is important in revealing the extent to which Shakespeare's plays question the prevailing attitudes. Consideration of what the play has to say about matters of social organisation or relationships between men and women can be explored most effectively, however, through analysis of the ways in which characters are presented and how their words and actions are judged within the text itself.

Language

By the time Shakespeare came to write *Othello*, he had already written about 25 plays. He was a skilled craftsman and experienced enough to be able to use language with supple versatility to serve a rich variety of dramatic effect. Throughout his career he used both verse and prose, with the proportions varying from play to play. *Richard II*, for example, is written entirely in verse, whereas *As You Like It* contains a very high proportion of prose. More usually, Shakespeare preferred to exploit both forms in a single play, giving himself greater flexibility to create characters with individual voices or to distinguish between formal, public scenes and moments of informal intimacy. Shifting between verse and prose can be a device which sharpens perceptions and encourages members of an audience to feel and think. At one moment they may identify with the individual confronting a dilemma, and then they will be prompted to reflect upon the epic dimension of a situation.

Verse

In favouring the medium of verse Shakespeare preferred to use lines which do not rhyme (blank verse) and have the pattern of five units (or feet) in which an unstressed syllable is followed by a stressed syllable, i.e. unrhymed, iambic pentameter. The English language is basically iambic (ti-tum) in its rhythms and, consequently, Shakespeare's verse can sound colloquial in preserving the natural rhythms of everyday speech. Iambic rhythms pattern the pulse that is fundamental to our sense of being alive. By using blank verse, Shakespeare helps an actor to share the heartbeat of an individual character. The rhythm is particularly useful for indicating tensions between thought and expression and for implying underlying motivations. Stanislavski's definition of subtext draws attention to the way in which performance requires a sense of the character's inner life:

> . . . the manifest, the inwardly-felt expression of a human being
> in a part, which flows uninterruptedly beneath the words of
> the text, giving them life and a basis for existing. The subtext is
> a web of innumerable varied inner patterns inside a play and a
> part, woven from magic 'ifs', the given circumstances, all sorts

of figments of the imagination, inner movements, objects of attention, smaller and greater truths and a belief in them, adaptations, adjustments and other similar elements. It is the subtext which makes us say the words we do in a play.

At times a speaker will contain his or her thoughts within a verse line, and what are called 'end-stopped lines' permit regular opportunities to take breath. Iago uses this device frequently, which is one reason why he appears straightforward and factual, decisive and unfussy:

> One Michael Cassio, a Florentine,
> A fellow almost damned in a fair wife,
> That never set a squadron in the field *(Act 1 Scene 1, lines 20–2)*

His lines often exploit a mid-line break, or *caesura*, to emphasise his plain-speaking:

> I know my price, I am worth no worse a place.
> *(Act 1 Scene 1, line 11)*

> Were I the Moor, I would not be Iago;
> In following him, I follow but myself. *(Act 1 Scene 1, lines 58–9)*

In contrast, the sense of an utterance can run over several lines, perhaps indicating pressure of feeling, fluency or confidence. Complicated thoughts and arguments cannot necessarily be contained and a character under emotional stress might be driven by impulses too strong to control. Othello's determination to remain committed to revenge is expressed in a sentence which spans eight lines of verse in which the relentless energy of the 'Pontic Sea' is exemplified:

> Like to the Pontic Sea,
> Whose icy current and compulsive course
> Ne'er feels retiring ebb but keeps due on
> To the Propontic and the Hellespont,
> Even so my bloody thoughts with violent pace
> Shall ne'er look back, ne'er ebb to humble love,
> Till that a capable and wide revenge
> Swallow them up. *(Act 3 Scene 3, lines 454–61)*

There is scarcely a chance to snatch breath in these lines. Othello is swept along by a force which is irresistibly powerful. The device of enjambement can also be used to reveal a character who is determinedly using the run-on lines as a means of preventing interruption. Othello's final speech demonstrates control both of himself and of his audience. After dealing clearly and concisely with his public service, the style modulates into a controlled, yet fluent and passionate account of the tragic events just witnessed by stage and theatre audiences.

Punctuation can alert a reader to the way the verse is working, but students do need to be wary of basing any argument upon the frequency or absence of commas, etc. The layout of a modern text reflects interpretative decisions taken by an editor and even the first published texts simply indicate the habits of the compositors rather than what the author wrote. In assessing how verse functions, the ear is more valuable than the eye. In a characteristically vigorous way, George Bernard Shaw asserted the need to respect the authority of the verse form:

> In playing Shakespear, play to the lines, through the lines, on the lines, but never between the lines. There simply isnt time for it. You would not stick five bars rest into a Beethoven symphony to pick up your drumsticks; and similarly you must not stop the Shakespear orchestra for business. Nothing short of a procession or a fight should make anything so extraordinary as a silence during a Shakespearean performance.

Verse enables Shakespeare to mark pauses or indicate silence. In a regular passage of verse, a line that is metrically deficient gives the character a pause. When Iago tells Roderigo how Othello ignored advice when appointing his lieutenant, he asks him:

And what was he? *(Act 1 Scene 1, line 18)*

The short line has only two feet. The absent three feet, therefore, offer three beats of silence to allow a dramatic pause before Iago gives the information. Short lines can also provide the space necessary for action. Othello announces:

> Look here, Iago,
> All my fond love thus do I blow to heaven;
> 'Tis gone.   *(Act 3 Scene 3, lines 445–7)*

The four beats of silence give the actor space for an extravagant gesture and time to look for a response.

The verse line also provides Shakespeare with a means of indicating how characters relate to each other through their dialogue. The effect of one character finishing half-way through a line of verse and another character completing it can be to demonstrate a harmony between characters who intuitively respond to each other's rhythms. They must pick up cues immediately so that separate speeches work together. When Othello and Desdemona meet in Cyprus (Act 2 Scene 1, lines 174–91), their speeches function in this way and culminate in a physical embodiment of such unity, a kiss.

However, the effect can be more disturbing. The central temptation scene (Act 3 Scene 3) has two long sections of dialogue between Othello and Iago. In the first (lines 90–259), Iago takes the lead and frequently completes Othello's half lines. Iago takes the initiative and is directing the course of their conversation. However, in the later section there is a reversal as Othello forces Iago onto the defensive (lines 334–480). The balance of power wavers and shifts until the nature of the partnership is secured. Their mutual commitment at the end of the scene is signalled by dovetailed speeches, the effect of which is reinforced by the ritual of kneeling together.

The rhythmic texture of a scene is created by the way in which the dialogue is distributed. There may be a balance, or one character may dominate. This is a characteristic of a play-text which can be lost when reading rather than seeing the play, and it can be too easy to ignore the presence of silent characters such as Emilia in the handkerchief scene (Act 3 Scene 4). Since the eye tends to anticipate, the reader always knows (until just before the page turn) how much more a particular character has to say. There is, therefore, a temptation to impose a sense of structure that is essentially non-dramatic. However, when a character begins to speak on stage, an audience cannot know whether it will be a short speech or an extended utterance. Theatre works moment-by-moment and long speeches are built – they do not appear on stage ready assembled. A lengthy speech can be delivered by a character who has a lot to say and is determined to say it. Alternatively, a character can keep speaking because others are unwilling to speak or have nothing to say.

In the senate scene (Act 1 Scene 3) it is easy to assume that Othello is lecturing the senators because his speech beginning 'Her father loved me . . .' is his longest speech in the play. However, when Othello was earlier urged to defend himself against Brabantio's accusations, his response was to request that Desdemona be brought, 'let her speak of me before her father'. The account he gives is only extended in so far as is necessary to fill in time 'till she come'. Othello's persuasive speech grows out of the rapt attentiveness of his on-stage audience and there is not necessarily the impression that he is adopting the role of a conscious orator. In contrast, Emilia's long speech in Act 4 Scene 3 has the effect of the character unburdening herself. She finds a voice, speaks at greater length than anywhere else in the play and the interest of her speech is primarily in what it reveals about the speaker and her attitude towards men. Although it evokes a powerful response from the audience it would seem, sadly, to say little to Desdemona.

The pace of such a sequence is very different from that created by dialogue which consists of a rapid exchange of single or even partial lines of verse, a device that is known as *stichomythia*. Such passages quicken the pace. The device works well for interrogation, such as when Othello questions Desdemona about the handkerchief:

> –   I'faith, is't true?
> – Most veritable; therefore look to't well.
> – Then would to God that I had never seen't!
> – Ha? Wherefore?
> – Why do you speak so startingly and rash?
> – Is't lost? Is't gone? Speak; is't out of th'way?
> – Heaven bless us!
> – Say you?
> – It is not lost, but what and if it were?
> – How?
> – I say it is not lost.   *(Act 3 Scene 4, lines 71–81)*

Othello uses the same device with Emilia in Act 4 Scene 2 (lines 1–10) and with Desdemona again in Act 5 Scene 2 (lines 23–85). It also works to create the sense of a flurry of activity as characters struggle to come to terms with a situation. In Act 5 Scene 1, the fragmented dialogue contributes to creating the uncertainty of darkness as Cassio is attacked and Iago uses the subsequent confusion to cover his tracks.

Although the majority of the play uses blank verse, rhyme is used by Iago to conclude his soliloquies. The effect is of a shaped and completed utterance which, perhaps misleadingly in this case, suggests a clarity of purpose. Othello arguably reveals Iago's influence when he uncharacteristically uses such a couplet in Act 5 Scene 1 (lines 35–6). The Duke's rhyming couplets reveal that he is more concerned with political expediency than with placating Brabantio. His words seem to come too easily and the trite rhymes suggest insincerity. Brabantio replies in the same style, revealing his awareness of the Duke's cynicism. Shakespeare enables Brabantio to express his bitterness through his conscious use of such a contrived style. He breaks out of it to indicate his awareness of the separation that is being signalled between concern for him and the political business, 'Beseech you now, to the affairs of the state.'

Rhyme can give statements a symbolic quality or a proverbial force. Desdemona's couplet at the end of Act 4 has the form almost of prayer. There is a solemn, even an ominous, note struck by the way the lines detach themselves from what has gone before:

> Good night, good night. God me such uses send,
> Not to pick bad from bad, but by bad mend!
>
> *(Act 4 Scene 3, lines 100–1)*

Prose

Although prose does not have the rhythmic pattern of verse, it can be analysed in just the same kind of detail as verse. There is clearly more flexibility about the delivery but, nevertheless, Shakespeare provides guidance to the actor through such matters as the diction, syntax and phrasing. The choice of words makes use of the same devices of alliteration, metaphor, etc. as verse. The shift from one form to another is a way in which the tone and mood of a scene can be changed. The notion that the distinction between verse and prose mirrors a class or hierarchical distinction has some validity in a play such as *King Henry IV Part 1* but it is not a feature of *Othello*. Most characters in this play use both forms. The only characters who speak exclusively in prose are the Clown, the Musicians and the Herald. The Clown's subtle punning suggests that he is an astute observer of those he serves. Like Feste in *Twelfth Night*, or Lear's Fool, he has a degree of detachment from events and the freedom of prose is well suited to convey a voice that is unconstrained. The Herald reads an announcement and there is no sense of his words being shaped by character. His clear prose alerts an audience to gain a perspective upon Othello's view of his role in Cyprus.

Iago is master of both verse and prose. He uses prose to re-establish Roderigo's trust at the end of Act 1 and in Act 2 Scene 1. Its flexibility gives the impression of informality and dispels any sense of his manipulation of his friend. But the repeated phrases 'put money in thy purse' offer an example of the way in which prose can reveal self-conscious shaping by the speaker even if it is not apparent to the person he is addressing. Prose creates the informality of the men's drinking scene (Act 2 Scene 3) and, similarly, its brief use in Act 4 Scene 3 suggests an emerging relaxation in the relationship between Desdemona and Emilia. Othello's only sustained prose speech signals his breakdown. It precedes his epileptic fit and fragmented speech effectively illustrates his loss of control, even before his physical collapse. In the 'overhearing' scene which follows, his interjections are also fragmentary, but perhaps most telling is the fact that his exchange with Iago after Bianca and Cassio's exit (Act 4 Scene 1, lines 162–200) is in prose and has something of the quality of Iago's previous exchanges with Roderigo.

Soliloquy

A character alone on stage has a privileged opportunity to forge a relationship with the audience. A soliloquy can be introspective as a character speaks aloud inner thoughts and feelings. Hamlet's soliloquies work in this way. But at other times, characters can speak directly to the audience, in a way which is challenging, confrontational, sinister, amusing or conspiratorial. Richard III opens his play with just this kind of direct address.

It is a particular quality of *Othello* that Shakespeare does not rely upon soliloquy in any substantial way in his presentation of the play's hero. Othello's opportunity for reflection in the middle of Act 3 Scene 3 is prevented when Iago fails to make his promised exit, thus allowing Othello only two lines:

Why did I marry? This honest creature doubtless
Sees and knows more, much more, than he unfolds.

(lines 244–5)

Only at the beginning of the last scene of the play does Othello have a sustained speech on his own and even here there is the silent figure of Desdemona on stage. Whether she is asleep or merely feigning sleep is a question which Suzanne Cloutier's performance in Orson Welles' film might prompt (see page 127).

In contrast, Iago has many soliloquies. The distinction in Shakespeare's dramatic method between the two characters has fuelled critical speculation about which is really the central role (see pages 92–3). There is a debate about which kind of soliloquy Iago offers. His direct presentation of commentary and strategy, which would seem to be telling the audience what he is doing, is thought by some commentators to be rich material for psychological inquiry. However, arguably, what Shakespeare achieves in this play is a paradoxical situation in which the soliloquy provides less insight into character than is gained by observation of the behaviour of the hero in a social context.

Desdemona and Emilia are each given brief moments alone on stage. In both cases, the women speak about their husbands. Desdemona's three lines come in the middle of Act 4 Scene 2 and suggest an isolation in her distress as she accepts her husband's cruelty to her. Emilia's ten-line speech when she finds the handkerchief (Act 3 Scene 3) provides evidence of the absolute priority she gives to her commitment to her husband.

Antithesis

The essence of drama is conflict, and in this play the opposition of character is demonstrated through the clash of different kinds of language. So, at the beginning of the play the weakness of Roderigo's 'Tush' is countered by Iago's ''Sblood'. Iago's crudity in referring to Othello's marriage, 'he tonight hath boarded a land carrack', is rejected by Cassio, whose reply, 'I do not understand', signals his distaste. Shakespeare uses antithesis not only to oppose characters but also philosophies. Throughout *Othello* Shakespeare sets 'hand' against 'heart' as he contrasts the importance of a code of honour with the imperative of personal commitment (see page 34).

Songs

Songs may be used dynamically to further the action. However, more usually in Shakespeare's plays they provide an opportunity for reflection upon situation or mood. They halt the propulsion of plot and enable members of an audience to take stock and crystallise their impressions. *Othello* makes use of both kinds of song.

There are two scenes in which characters are required to sing. The first is in Act 2 Scene 3 when Iago encourages a party atmosphere. His first song, 'And let me the cannikin clink, clink', actively promotes conviviality and directly serves Iago's purpose. The words create pressure on Cassio by asserting that drinking is a soldierly and a manly activity. He endorses 'an excellent song' and urges others to drink 'To the health of our general'.

The choice of Iago's other song may be interpreted as a reflection of a bitter resentment of his social inequality. The second stanza explicitly sets 'high renown' against 'low degree' and concludes:

> 'Tis pride that pulls the country down;
> Then take thine auld cloak about thee.
>
> *(Act 2 Scene 3, lines 82–3)*

Moments later, Cassio declares his sense of his own superiority when he announces that 'the lieutenant is to be saved before the ancient'.

The final song occurs in Act 4 Scene 3 when Desdemona invokes a memory of her past through a song she remembers her mother's maid, Barbary, singing. Before Desdemona sings, an audience is prompted to consider the significance of the song through the details Desdemona herself gives about its history:

> She had a song of willow;
> An old thing 'twas but it expressed her fortune,
> And she died singing it. That song tonight
> Will not go from my mind. *(Act 4 Scene 3, lines 27–30)*

Imagery

Imagery can provide insight into the ways in which a character sees the world or relates to others. It also works upon the audience to stimulate a visual dimension to the process of experiencing the play. This was particularly important in Shakespeare's theatre because there was neither scenery nor the possibility of lighting effects. At the beginning of *Henry V*, the Chorus establishes the necessary contract with the audience and urges:

> On your imaginary forces work.
> . . .
> Piece out our imperfections with your thoughts.
> . . .
> And make imaginary puissance.
> Think when we talk of horses that you see them
> Printing their proud hoofs i'th'receiving earth
>
> *(Prologue, lines 18, 23, 25–7)*

The theatrical experience requires the creative cooperation of the audience in order that 'the flat, unraised spirits', the actors, can convincingly play their parts.

The marriage of black and white is at the heart of *Othello* and the play's imagery repeatedly exploits the juxtaposition. Conventional assumptions about the goodness of that which is white, virginal and pure are opposed to the stereotyped connections between blackness, corruption and evil. Iago describes how he is intent upon turning Desdemona's 'virtue' into 'pitch', her purity into the blackness of tar. Othello reveals Iago's success not only by the way he believes in Desdemona's infidelity but also by the way he speaks of it. He has succumbed to Iago's influence and he uses his frame of reference when he says:

> Her name, that was as fresh
> As Dian's visage, is now begrimed and black
> As mine own face.   *(Act 3 Scene 3, lines 387–9)*

The play's shift from night to day, indicated through the language, patterns the contrast. The first explicit reference to the marriage is provided by Iago when he tells Brabantio that 'an old black ram / Is tupping your white ewe'. When Brabantio confronts Othello, he expresses his disbelief that his 'fair' daughter would 'Run . . . to the sooty bosom / Of such a thing as thou'. The language also conveys these characters' attitudes to Othello's 'otherness'. Iago is implying Othello is bestial and Brabantio's use of 'thing' dehumanises Othello and excludes him from Brabantio's world.

Early in the play, Othello effectively counteracts such accusations through his own imagery. His language is exotic and extraordinary in ways which excite and fascinate. Just as Desdemona had been wooed by the experiences which opened up another world to her, an audience is fascinated by Othello's 'travels' history'. Although he judges himself 'rude' in speech he demonstrates an eloquence as he talks of

> . . . the cannibals that each other eat,
> The Anthropophagi, and men whose heads
> Do grow beneath their shoulders.   (Act 1 Scene 3, lines 142–4)

His words persuade the on-stage and theatre audiences and effectively counter Brabantio's accusation that Othello must have used 'foul charms', 'drugs or minerals' to steal Desdemona from her father.

There is a sustained opposition in the play between Iago's insistence that love is 'merely a lust of the blood and a permission of the will' and the spiritual dimension which informs the way in which Othello and Desdemona speak of their commitment to each other. Desdemona uses religious imagery when she appears in front of the senate and announces 'to his honours and his valiant parts / Did I my soul and fortunes consecrate'. Othello echoes the solemnity of her frame of reference, using the words 'heaven' and 'good souls'. When they are reunited in Cyprus, Othello greets her as 'my soul's joy' and Desdemona appeals to the 'heavens' that their 'loves and comforts' might increase. She maintains her faith both in Othello and in a spiritual realm. Her response to the change in Othello is to pray 'O, heaven forgive us!' She reaffirms her love 'by this light of heaven' and offers supplication, 'Here I kneel'.

Iago consistently projects his view of sexuality onto the marriage of Othello and Desdemona. He referred to them 'making the beast with two backs' to inflame Brabantio, and he persuades Othello through similarly vivid language to picture all too vividly Desdemona's infidelity. Even if she and Cassio were 'as prime as goats, as hot as monkeys', Othello could not expect to 'see her topped'. Iago's influence upon Othello is revealed as he leaves the stage (in Act 4 Scene 1) exclaiming, 'Goats and monkeys!'

Othello loses his own distinctive voice in the confusion that engulfs him. He becomes brutal ('I will chop her into messes') and he redefines his relationship with his wife as one in which a man visits a brothel. His 'soul's joy' becomes a 'cunning whore' or 'impudent strumpet'. When, in the final scene of the play, he realises how mistaken he has been, he regains his voice. His characteristic imagery is reasserted as Desdemona becomes the 'pearl . . . / Richer than all his tribe' which he foolishly 'threw' away. His 'subdued eyes' shed tears 'as fast as the Arabian trees / Their medicinable gum.'

Patterns of imagery reinforce the themes of the play, indicate the values and perspectives of individual characters and can demonstrate the ways in which allegiances between characters can change. Emilia echoes her husband's outlook when she talks of men being 'stomachs' which 'eat [women] hungerly' and 'belch' them when they are 'full'. But at the end of the play she will transfer her allegiance to the truth embodied by Desdemona and ask to be laid 'by my mistress' side'. Not only does she then echo her song 'Willow, willow, willow' but she aligns herself with Desdemona as she prays:

So come my soul to bliss, as I speak true

(Act 5 Scene 2, line 248)

Traditional criticism

The power of *Othello* in the theatre is such that it can seem to defy or render unnecessary the kind of exposition offered by critical writing. The play has proved to be one of the most consistently popular of all Shakespeare's plays on stage. It has a sustained and rich stage history and it would seem not to need the assistance of critical insight to make a case for it or to revive interest in it. As Samuel Johnson wrote in 1765, 'The beauties of this play impress themselves so strongly upon the attention of the reader, that they can draw no aid from critical illustration'. However, 'critical illustration' can usefully provide a sounding board for ideas, can stimulate other thoughts, can challenge and extend responses which may otherwise become blinkered.

One of the earliest pieces of critical writing on the play was offered in 1693 by Thomas Rymer. He was irritated by a play which seemed to lack any moral purpose and he mocked how prominently the handkerchief features in the plot:

> So much ado, so much stress, so much passion and repetition about an Handkerchief! Why was not this call'd the *Tragedy of the Handkerchief*? Had it been Desdemona's Garter the sagacious Moor might have smelt a Rat but the Handkerchief is so remote a trifle . . .

Rymer spectacularly missed the point. His use of the word 'trifle' is of course prompted by Shakespeare, though Rymer would seem to have had little appreciation of how it is used in its context. At the structural heart of the play Iago is able to exploit how

> Trifles light as air
> Are to the jealous confirmations strong
> As proofs of holy writ.   *(Act 3 Scene 3, lines 323–5)*

To view the play simply as a tragedy of misunderstanding inevitably is to trivialise it. Rymer satirised the play's lack of moral weight by suggesting that it offers three lessons: that 'Maidens of Quality' should not 'run away with Blackamoors', 'good wives' should 'look well to their linen' and husbands ensure that before their jealousy become 'tragical' the proof is 'mathematical'. He concluded that the play was 'a Bloody farce, without salt or savour'.

Writing in the early years of the nineteenth century, Hazlitt's response to the play exposed the paucity of Rymer's judgement. Hazlitt appreciated, and was able to analyse, the richness of the play's impact:

> Tragedy creates a balance of the affections. It makes us thoughtful spectators in the lists of life. It is the refiner of the species; a discipline of humanity . . . Othello furnishes an illustration of these remarks. It excites our sympathy in an extraordinary degree. The moral it conveys has a closer application to the concerns of human life than almost any other of Shakespear's plays.

He developed his argument through close and detailed consideration of character and, like Coleridge before him, he was fascinated by Iago. However, where Coleridge had attributed 'motiveless malignity' to Iago, Hazlitt refuted this vigorously. Shakespeare, he argued, understood human nature:

> He knew that the love of power, which is another name for the love of mischief, is natural to man. He would know this . . . merely from seeing children paddle in the dirt or kill flies for sport. Iago . . . belongs to a class of character . . . whose heads are as acute and active as their hearts are hard and callous.

Both Coleridge and Hazlitt responded to the deep and moving pathos of the play's tragic outcome, and their writing on the play was informed by a spiritual dimension. Coleridge saw Desdemona as an 'angel' who becomes 'sanctified', so she and Othello have a 'holy entireness of love'. Hazlitt saw Othello's passion 'heaved up from the bottom of the soul'. However, both critics revealed their intellectual fascination with the character of Iago.

The critic with whom the expression 'character study' is most associated is A C Bradley. Around 100 years ago, Bradley delivered a series of lectures at Oxford University which were published in 1904 as *Shakespearean Tragedy*. The book has never been out of print, and Bradley's approach has been hugely influential. It expressed the spirit of much nineteenth-century criticism, and it determined the form of the majority of criticism for a good deal of the twentieth century.

Bradley wrote of the characters in the play as if they were real people existing in worlds recognisable to modern readers. It is significant that he discusses Othello and Desdemona together in one lecture and devotes virtually all his second lecture on the play to Iago. He judges the character of Othello to be 'comparatively simple' whereas he lists Iago with Falstaff, Hamlet and Cleopatra as 'the most wonderful' of Shakespeare's characters.

Bradley argued that the noble Moor is defeated by the machinations of a villainous but fascinating Iago. He asserts that the play shows Iago's character in action and that 'any man situated as Othello was would have been disturbed by Iago's communications, and . . . many men would have been made wildly jealous'. Bradley was developing established critical opinion and he can be seen to endorse Coleridge's view of the play's tragic outcome:

> . . . that Othello does not kill Desdemona in jealousy but in a
> conviction forced upon him by the almost superhuman art of
> Iago, such a conviction as any man would and must have
> entertained who had believed Iago's honesty as Othello did.

Bradley's view has been enormously influential but it has also been emphatically challenged, resulting in an energetic and engaging debate.

First, T S Eliot, writing in 1927, challenged the notion of a 'noble Moor' and argued in particular that in his last speech Othello is

> . . . cheering himself up. He is endeavouring to escape reality,
> he has ceased to think about Desdemona and is thinking about
> himself . . . Othello succeeds in turning himself into a pathetic
> figure, by adopting an aesthetic rather than a moral attitude,
> dramatising himself against his environment.

Eliot's view of the play was sensitively developed by F R Leavis, who considered Othello's love to be 'a matter of self-centred and self-regarding satisfactions – pride, sensual possessiveness, appetite, love of loving'.

Both critics believed that to give a priority to Iago's character and to attempt to justify his actions in psychological terms is to displace the play's centre. Leavis published his refutation as *Diabolic Intellect and the Noble Hero: or The Sentimentalist's Othello*. He denounces Bradley's section on Othello as 'completely wrong-headed – grossly and palpably false to the evidence it offers to weigh'. Leavis states directly that 'in Shakespeare's tragedy of *Othello*, Othello is the chief personage – the chief personage in such a sense that the tragedy may fairly be said to be Othello's character in action.' His view of Othello's character is that he is an egoist prone to self-dramatisation. In putting Othello, therefore, unequivocally at the centre of his play, Leavis argues that 'Iago is subordinate and merely ancillary . . . He is not much more than a necessary piece of dramatic mechanism'. It is Othello's character and not Iago's which provokes the tragedy, for 'the essential traitor is within the gates'. In Leavis' view:

> Othello yields with extraordinary promptness to suggestion, with such promptness as to make it plain that the mind that undoes him is not Iago's but his own.

The critical quest to provide Iago with a motive and to focus such attention upon him can result in Othello becoming merely a victim.

Another way of challenging Bradley is that offered by G Wilson Knight. His book, *The Wheel of Fire*, offers an analysis of the play entitled 'The *Othello* Music'. He states quite simply that 'Othello is dominated by its protagonist' and argues that 'in first analysing Othello's poetry, we shall lay the basis for an understanding of the play's symbolism'. Such sensitive analysis redefines the character opposition of Othello and Iago as 'the spirit of negation set against the spirit of creation'. Iago is 'a colourless and ugly thing in a world of colour and harmony'.

A different approach to the language of the play is taken by William Empson. The words 'honest' and 'honesty' are used 52 times in *Othello*, and Empson offers a searching and meticulous examination of the implications and effect of what he judges to be a unique device. For, he states, there is no other play in which Shakespeare 'worries a word like that'. A more wide-ranging analysis of the imagery of the play is offered by Caroline Spurgeon in her book, *Shakespeare's*

Imagery and What it Tells Us. She identifies image-clusters as a dominant feature of the plays, arguing that the recurrence of such clusters is a crucial means by which the particular atmosphere or mood of a play is created. In *Othello*, she draws attention to the importance of imagery of animals, of the sea and of poisoning.

The domestic aspects of *Othello* have prompted consideration of some ways in which the play might be seen to exploit elements more usually found in comedy. B H de Mendonca's article '*Othello*: A Tragedy Built on a Comic Structure' identifies the structural links between Othello and the characteristics of *commedia dell'arte*. She focuses upon the role of the traditional *zanni* figure, who is the mischievous engine of the complex plotting that characterises the improvised plays performed by the travelling Italian players. She argues that in *Othello*, Iago as *zanni*

> ... spinning his web of lies, not only gets caught in it himself but sets in motion passions which he could neither feel emotionally nor understand intellectually. For once, in his long and varied career, Zanni blunders into a world of tragedy, but it took Shakespeare to see the full theatrical possibilities of such a blunder.

The tradition of character criticism continues and, indeed, underlies much of what is termed 'modern critical approaches'. Jane Adamson's book '*Othello' as Tragedy* (1980) sets out to explore why the play has so starkly polarised critical debate along the lines established by Bradley and Leavis. Ultimately she rejects both readings, urging instead an acknowledgement of the complex way in which the play examines how relationships are fraught with uncertainty and damaged by doubt. She rejects the impulse to judge the characters in moral terms, which she identifies as central to both Bradley and Leavis, arguing rather that the experience of the play makes its audience 'acutely aware of our own needs for emotional and moral certainty, simplicity and finality' as a way of lessening the 'full brunt of the tragedy'.

The ferocity with which the debate about the relative importance of Othello and Iago has been fought traditionally meant that Desdemona came a very poor third in terms of the attention paid to her character and situation. Marvin Rosenberg grants her a chapter in his study, *The Masks of Othello*. He explains that 'this loveliest of heroines needs a champion, not only against the criticism of her detractors, but also against the dangerous praise of some of her friends'. In declaring that she does 'indeed tell a lie', Rosenberg vigorously defends her human frailty, though other critics have been less charitable. In *The Critics' Debate: 'Othello'*, Peter Davison records the worries that have been expressed about the impact that her 'free and open nature' that 'is sensual' has upon men other than her husband. Even her defenders insist that Desdemona must take some responsibility for her fate. Rosenberg's view is that 'Desdemona is a fine woman, a fair woman, a sweet woman driven by fear and love to untruth' and, albeit with some reluctance, Stanley Wells, in *Shakespeare: A Dramatic Life*, apportions blame: 'And it must be confessed that Desdemona contributes to her own downfall, above all in the innocent but ill-judged pertinacity with which she nags Othello to forgive Cassio.'

Feminist criticism

Feminist criticism is part of the wider feminist movement which aims to achieve rights and equality for women in political, social and economic life. It challenges sexism, those beliefs and practices which result in the degradation, oppression and subordination of women. Feminist criticism therefore challenges traditional portrayals of female characters as examples of 'virtue' or 'vice' or more particularly in *Othello* as 'virgin' or 'whore'. It rejects 'male ownership' of criticism in which men determined what questions were to be asked of a play, and which answers were acceptable. Feminism therefore argues that male criticism often neglects, represses or misrepresents female experience, and stereotypes or distorts the women's point of view.

The domestic dimension of *Othello* and its concern with marital relationships and sexuality, which has sometimes encouraged a somewhat patronising attitude to its range and achievement, has prompted rich and perceptive work by critics interested in the issue of gender in Shakespeare. In particular, there are good individual chapters on *Othello* in the following: Coppélia Kahn, *Man's Estate: Masculine Identity in Shakespeare* (1981), Marianne Novy, *Love's Argument: Gender Relations in Shakespeare* (1984) and Carol Thomas Neely, *Broken Nuptials in Shakespeare's Plays* (1985). Most feminist studies of Shakespeare include consideration of *Othello's* exploration of the women's world. As Evelyn Gajowski argues, 'Shakespeare represents in *Othello* the reality of women – their wholeness – in high contrast to the fragmented notions of them held by men.'

It is frequently argued that the handkerchief 'spotted with strawberries' carries weighty sexual symbolism. It has been seen to represent the stained wedding sheets and, therefore, embody evidence of Othello and Desdemona's marital bond, and yet also display how the purity of their love is marred. However, the way in which the handkerchief binds the women is important.

The three women in *Othello* are united in that they each at different times hold the handkerchief 'spotted with strawberries'. The flimsiness of what Othello takes to be 'ocular proof' of Desdemona's infidelity also functions as a symbol of the women's failure to recognise that what they have in common is greater than what divides them. During the course of the play, the handkerchief passes through the hands of Desdemona, Othello, Emilia, Iago, Cassio and Bianca without any of the three women knowing how it serves to connect them. For each of the women, the handkerchief is only important because of its function in relationship to the men they love. Desdemona, Emilia and Bianca each allow the priority they give to the marital bond to distract them from what they have in common with each other.

The handkerchief was given to Othello by his mother, who had it from an Egyptian woman. It was then his first gift to Desdemona and, solicitous for his 'pain upon [his] forehead', she sought to use her napkin to 'bind it'. He pushes it away and Emilia picks it up. She knows its importance to her mistress and yet she gives it to Iago in an attempt to please 'his fantasy'. Bianca becomes suspicious when Cassio gives her the handkerchief, certain that it is 'some minx's token'. It is returned defiantly. Bianca is determined not to be exploited although, like Desdemona and Emilia, she loves a man who treats her badly. She is not legally bound to Cassio, but she has an emotional commitment which prevents her from severing their relationship. So, after Othello had given the handkerchief to Desdemona it passes from her to Emilia, then via Iago and Cassio to Bianca. The 'magic in the web of it' was designed to keep the husband happy. Othello's account of its history recognises the frailty of a man's faith, and the instability of the masculine gaze: the 'eye' can so easily 'hold her loathed'. What is recognised is the potential for male, rather than female, infidelity.

An awareness of the handkerchief's structural contribution to the play might challenge conventional judgements upon Desdemona, Emilia and Bianca. Even in much feminist criticism the prevalent view is that the female characters in *Othello* represent three kinds of women separated by a clearly defined social and moral hierarchy. Virginia Mason Vaughan identified the gradations as a 'spectrum of female sexual mores . . . with Bianca the prostitute, Emilia the earthy matron, and Desdemona the chaste bride'. The assumption generally is that Emilia and Bianca contrast with Desdemona rather than provide parallel patterns. Even in as sensitive and thoughtful an analysis as that offered by Eamon Grennan, Bianca is described as 'difficult and tough, and can be unpleasant'. The critic seems almost disappointed that 'she is not, however, the whore with the heart of gold', implying perhaps that such a stereotype would be preferable.

The journey of the handkerchief links Bianca with Desdemona and Emilia. The play's structure charts the waste of constant, loving women underestimated and abused by the men they love. The real tragedy for Desdemona, Emilia and Bianca is the way their marital and emotional bonding pre-empts or takes precedence over their common cause. In one sense, Rymer could be said to be right. The handkerchief is 'so remote a trifle' that it is absurd that it should have such power to destroy trust between people who love each other. But Iago exploited the ease with which a man's eye can so easily 'hold her loathed'. With clear-sighted astuteness, Emilia ultimately explodes the myth of any intrinsic power in the handkerchief and she herself pre-empts Rymer's complaint. The 'solemn earnestness' attached to the handkerchief is, she declares, 'More than indeed belonged to such a trifle' (Act 5 Scene 2, line 226).

Performance criticism

Performance criticism engages with the insight that can be gained from exploration of the transition from page to stage. In the past, performance was seen as separate from intellectual analysis of the text. Staging the plays was sometimes seen as a process which not only denied an intrinsic subtlety but in some ways coarsened the experience provided by Shakespeare's text. Charles Lamb drew a clear distinction between the experience of reading and seeing *Othello*:

Nothing can be more soothing, more flattering to the nobler
parts of our natures, than to read of a young Venetian lady of
the highest extraction, through the force of love and from a
sense of merit in him whom she loved, laying aside every
consideration of kindred, and country, and colour, and
wedding with a coal-black Moor . . . She sees Othello's colour
in his mind. But upon the stage, when the imagination is no
longer the ruling faculty, but we are left to our poor unassisted
senses, I appeal to every one that has seen Othello played . . .
whether he did not find something extremely revolting in the
courtship and wedded caresses of Othello and Desdemona;
and whether the actual sight of the thing did not over-weigh
all the beautiful compromise which we make in reading . . .
What we see upon a stage is body and bodily action; what we
are conscious of in reading is almost exclusively the mind, and
its movements; and this I think may sufficiently account for the
very different sort of delight with which the same play so often
affects us in the reading and the seeing.

Although Lamb has a general distaste for the vulgarity of
performance, his words here reveal a particular distaste for the
physicalising of the relationship between a black Othello and a white
Desdemona. His reaction is testament not only to his prejudice but
also to the enduring nature of Shakespeare's incisive challenging of
received opinion in crafting the play.

Despite Lamb's resistance *Othello* has proved one of the most
consistently popular of Shakespeare's plays, with a vigorous,
sustained and exciting stage history. The first recorded performance
of *Othello* was in 1604:

By the Kings Maiesties plaiers. Hallamas Day being the first of
Nouember A Play in the Banketinge House att WhitHall Called
the Moor of Venis.

There are records of it being presented again in April 1610, at the
Globe, and in September of the same year at Oxford. There were court
performances in 1612–13, 1629, 1635 and 1636. When the theatres
were re-opened in 1660, after the Civil War, two performances of
Othello were staged immediately and it is generally believed that the

first appearance of an actress on the English stage was as Desdemona. Samuel Pepys recorded his enjoyment of a performance:

> To the Cockpit to see 'The Moor of Venice', which was well done. Burt acted the Moor: by the same token, a very pretty lady that sat by me called out, to see Desdemona smothered.
>
> Samuel Pepys, *Diary*, 11 October, 1660

The play continued to be popular despite heavy cutting to suit Restoration tastes.

Thomas Betterton played Othello in 1683, and Richard Steele noted (as Pepys had done before him) the necessary and added dimension given by performance as against the 'dry, incoherent, and broken sentences' found by a reader. Steele was impressed by Betterton's moving and graceful energy, and by 'the wonderful agony . . . when he examined the circumstance of the handkerchief . . . the mixture of love that intruded upon his mind upon the innocent answers Desdemona makes'. One of David Garrick's greatest achievements was his Iago. His Othello (in 1745), however, was not a success, though he did restore the epileptic scene and added a turban to Othello's customary British Army uniform. Throughout the whole of the eighteenth century, there were only seven years in which there was no London performance. The play's popularity continued and in 1785, and through the early years of the nineteenth century, John Philip Kemble was giving carefully controlled, meticulous and dignified performances. His sister, Sarah Siddons, played Desdemona, giving an 'importance to the character which it never possessed before'.

The greatest Othello was Edmund Kean (1787–1833). 'To see him act,' said Coleridge, 'is like reading Shakespeare by flashes of lightning.' First impressions were unprepossessing. Kean was variously described as a little ill-looking vagabond, a pot-house actor with a low and meagre figure and a hoarse voice, somewhat between an apoplexy and a cold, and his performances did not suit the purists who had praised Kemble. But in the huge theatres of the time, Kean had the breadth of effect necessary to communicate an intense reality.

The night after his initial success as Othello (on 5 May 1814), he gave an almost equally brilliant interpretation of Iago, and alternated the parts for several seasons. Once, a young actor by the name of

Lucius Junius Brutus Booth was rash enough to challenge Kean's pre-eminence by playing Kean's parts in the Kean manner. Kean invited him to play Iago to his own Othello. Booth was devastatingly upstaged and before the advertised second encounter he literally ran away and hid.

For many years, subsequent Othellos were overshadowed by Kean's performance. In 1875, Thomaso Salvini (acting in Italian amidst an English-speaking cast) was the first Othello to strike his Desdemona. The power and dignity of his interpretation prompted the American novelist Henry James to judge him the perfect Othello, and indeed from the time of Kean to that of Olivier there has been a general reluctance to believe English actors capable of the part. Irving, Forbes-Robertson, Ralph Richardson and John Gielgud all failed, whereas, according to Kenneth Tynan's vigorous, provocative and shocking account, Frederick Valk came near in 1947:

> What paroxysms of fright and foreboding must have
> consumed Shakespeare's Jacobean audiences! Here, proudly
> booming before them, was a monstrous blackamoor, a black
> gargoyle, concealing within him racks on which to stretch
> himself and those about him until the excruciated lyric cry was
> released; and bearing in his baggage explosive coils of taut,
> dangerous springs. Anything might happen while this nigger
> devil yet lived. Horrors and Domdaniel excesses crowded the
> horizon. I had never fully shared this expectancy of terror until
> Mr Valk pressed me, at pistol point, to accept it.

The play's popularity has crossed national boundaries – for instance in Russia, between 1945 and 1957, there were 78 different productions. The Russian passion for the play reached a climax in 1964, when 15 separate productions were mounted.

In recent years, however, *Othello* has been performed comparatively rarely, and to some extent the paucity of productions is the result of the imprint Laurence Olivier put upon the part in the National Theatre production directed by John Dexter in 1964. In theatrical terms Olivier's Othello came so close to being universally acclaimed as definitive that since 1964 actors and directors have approached the play comparatively rarely and then only with considerable trepidation.

As has been indicated, critical discussion throughout the twentieth century has been obsessed with the rival claims to centre-stage of Othello and Iago. It was the prevalence of Bradley's view that made Olivier initially cautious about playing Othello when the 1964 National Theatre production was suggested. He felt that one of the main problems was the 'awful loading against the role by the author's delight in Iago'. He had played Iago in 1938, causing a stir by exploring aspects of the homo-erotic in the relationship between Iago and Othello. Olivier thought that his voice lacked the 'violet velvet' that the role of Othello demanded and it was only after rigorous vocal and physical training that he felt fit for the part. He sought to restore Othello's position in the play and, influenced by Leavis' argument, Olivier rejected the traditional view of the truly noble man who was jealous and gullible, believing that Othello was 'only a goodish fellow who had merely fixed the earmark of nobility upon himself'. The tragic flaw in Othello's character was his self-delusion.

Such was the impact of the production, and the demand for tickets, that there was enormous pressure to capture it on film. Writing in the *New Statesman*, Ronald Bryden was in no doubt of the importance of what had been created:

> . . . we had seen history, and it was over. Perhaps it's as well to have seen the performance while still unripe, constructed in fragments, still knitting itself. Now you can see how it's done; later, it will be a torrent. But before it exhausts him a film should be made. It couldn't save the whole truth, but it might save something the unborn should know.

It was filmed in a studio and directed by Stuart Burge. However, the shape and movements of the theatre production were retained and at no time was a script used. The film provides a record of a remarkable stage production. Olivier later expressed some dissatisfaction with his own performance:

> Alas, my performance was tired. I mistimed effects. Somehow I was lacking in confidence and full vitality; perhaps, subconsciously, I was being gnawed by the question: 'Why aren't we making a full-blown Shakespeare film of this?' Certainly I regret that now.

Olivier's words acknowledge that what was captured on film was a record of a stage production and that accounts for the 'theatricality' of its style. But, nevertheless, it offers those too young to have seen the production in the theatre an opportunity to share something of the experience of a quite remarkable performance. The influence of Leavis' writing on the play is apparent in Olivier's performance, which shows Othello's propensity to self-dramatisation, a vanity, even a sense of racial superiority which makes his disintegration all the more terrible to witness. Frank Finlay's Iago exploits the power of close-up. Despite intense scrutiny, there is a coldness behind the eyes which powerfully embodies his statement 'what you know, you know'. However imperfect the experience might be, there is undoubted value in capturing theatrical performances on film.

Janet Suzman's 1988 production was the first time the play had been performed in South Africa with a black Othello and a white Desdemona. The television version provides compelling evidence of the political dimension of the play. It reveals terrible contemporary resonances to a world in which the racist attitudes expressed by some in the play can still exist. Iago's racism is ugly and disturbing. Alone on stage after the scene in which Othello has struck Desdemona in front of Lodovico, Iago looks out at the audience and then grins sickeningly as he echoes Othello's cry of 'Goats and monkeys!' He bends forward to let his arms hang ape-like, parodying what he suggests is Othello's primal inferiority.

More recently, notions of political correctness have prompted expressed anxieties about a white actor 'blacking-up' to play Othello. The pre-publicity for Trevor Nunn's 1989 production in Stratford-upon-Avon's studio theatre used such arguments to justify the importation of Willard White into the Royal Shakespeare Company. The Wagnerian power of a singer more accustomed to the vastness of the world's opera houses was cast against a Iago played by Ian McKellen, an actor thoroughly experienced in making small detail read expressively in intimate spaces such as The Other Place. Willard White was wholly out of his element and the play was effectively surrendered to Iago before rehearsals started. It could be argued that the engineering of a theatrical imbalance was more offensive racially than the integrity of interpretations such as those by Alan Badel for the Oxford Stage Company in 1970 and by Ben Kingsley for the RSC in 1985, as well as those by Welles, Bondarchuk and Olivier (see page 127).

Any performance is shaped in its creation by its culture and attitudes will inevitably shift and evolve. In evaluating performances from the past it is vital to take account of the ways in which contemporary audiences responded and of the judgements made at the time of the performances. In this respect, reviews, eye-witness accounts by those who were there in the theatre at the time the performances were created, are invaluable sources of insight and information. In recent years there have been comparatively few opportunities to see the play performed on stage. It has sadly become a widespread view that only black actors should play the role and some black actors do not wish to play Othello because they feel the role is a racist stereotype. Perhaps it is time to break free from the shackles of a constraining naturalism and let the power of the language do the kind of work that it did in Shakespeare's theatre.

In 1994, Kim Brandstrup choreographed a ballet version which indicated Othello's 'otherness' not through the colour of his skin but through the contrast established by the casting of a single classical dancer in a modern dance company. The exhilarating possibilities of *pas de deux*, when these two worlds came together in the marriage of Othello and Desdemona (created by Irek Mukhamedov and Leesa Phillips), provided a brilliant correlative for the excitement and aspiration of Shakespeare's text.

Performance criticism is one of the most important recent developments in analytical approaches to Shakespeare's plays. It explores Shakespeare's stagecraft and the semiotics of theatre (signs, words, costumes, gestures, etc.) but, crucially, it is an acknowledgement that the best performances are like the best critical writing upon a text in providing insight and prompting fresh thoughts about the ways in which the plays work today. An early and very influential critic was Harley Granville Barker, himself an actor, playwright and director. His *Prefaces to Shakespeare* approach the plays in a theatrically pragmatic way, offering a commentary upon the text which draws attention to the ways in which the action is shaped and a consistent exploration of the implications for staging. He emphasises the need to engage with the implications of the bare stage for which Shakespeare was writing. For example, he offers the following thoughts on how Iago comments upon the way Cassio is talking to Desdemona whilst waiting for Othello to arrive:

Iago emerges from the picture (the action must be thought of in terms of Shakespeare's stage) for his malignly vigilant soliloquy:

> He takes her by the palm. Ay, well said, whisper; with as
> little a web as this, will I ensnare so great a fly as Cassio . . .

and her share of the scene is reduced to illustrative dumb show; but since she is the subject of the soliloquy she still will hold our attention. The scene's action is here momentarily split, so to speak, into two, its force isolated in the menacingly prominent figure of Iago. Upon his dry explicatory prose the brilliant interruption of the *Trumpet within* tells the more startlingly.

An increasing number of books celebrate the excitement and insight provided in the theatre. John Russell Brown's *Shakespeare's Plays in Performance* shows how description and analysis can go hand in hand, particularly paying tribute to 'the huge opportunities Shakespeare has provided for an actor who is at once realistic and histrionic . . . Olivier's performance was supremely inventive, sustained and astonishing'. Marvin Rosenberg's *The Masks of 'Othello'* offers a thorough and painstakingly detailed account of the ways in which twentieth-century productions have interpreted the play. More selective in its examples is Martin L Wine's volume on *Othello* in the Macmillan Text and Performance series. He focuses upon the performances with Paul Robeson (1943–4), Laurence Olivier (1964), Brewster Mason (1971–2) and James Earl Jones (1981–2). The format of Julie Hankey's volume on *Othello* in the Plays in Performance series offers, like a promptbook, the text of the play faced by details of the ways in which the play has been staged and interpreted moment by moment. It facilitates comparisons between interpretations and the layout acknowledges the value for work on stage history of the evidence provided by promptbooks.

There is a rich combination of performance study and an historicist approach in Virginia Mason Vaughan, *Othello: A Contextual History*. The second section of the book traces the history of performances of *Othello* in England and the United States from the Restoration to the late 1980s. Rather than seek to be comprehensive in its coverage, it offers detailed accounts of some particular productions and the stated aim is

> . . . to historicize, to place the *Othello* of a particular generation
> and culture within its historical framework and to demonstrate
> why elements from the original text(s) were emphasised or
> repressed. . . . My goal is to show *Othello* not simply as a
> product of a cultural milieu but also as a maker of cultural
> meanings, part of a complex negotiation between each
> episteme's cultural attitudes, its actors and their audiences.

There are full and detailed accounts of the productions of *Othello* with Paul Robeson, Orson Welles and Willard White in the title role.

Unfortunately most books dealing with performance are woefully short of illustration. However, Kenneth Tynan's book entitled *'Othello': The National Theatre Production* offers a record of John Dexter's production (with Olivier as Othello) at the National Theatre through a remarkable sequence of black-and-white photographs offering real insight into the moment-by-moment experience of the production. An essay by Tynan begins with the sentence 'My theme is the growth of a performance.' There are also reviews and, as acknowledgement of the influence upon Olivier's interpretation, an extract from Leavis' article is included. In a lavishly illustrated book entitled *Shakespeare in Performance* there is a chapter by the present writer analysing *Othello* in terms of its theatrical and interpretative possibilities. The article is supported by film stills and numerous photographs of stage productions.

Study of Shakespeare on film has proliferated in recent years and there is an increasing acknowledgement of the need to analyse film versions of Shakespeare's plays with a recognition of the demands of the medium. An annotated list of available screen versions is provided on page 127. Cutting and shaping of Shakespeare's text is inevitable in the process of making a screenplay out of a theatrical text. Orson Welles' *Othello* has been recently re-released and it offers a compelling interpretation of the play. Welles' decision about how to begin the film departs from Shakespeare's text, but using the very different vocabulary of film his approach has a compelling integrity:

> The opening shots of the funeral procession express the
> inevitability of tragedy. But the projected title page, which is
> also read to us, acknowledges the dimension of narrative and
> gives the story the perspective of time. The film, true to the

play, allows Othello to be introduced through Iago's uncomplimentary perspective. At first we are given only glimpses of Othello; in a gondola, the back of a turbaned head, a figure descending a staircase. With Brabantio's impassioned disbelief that his daughter would 'run from her father to the sooty-bosom of such a thing as that' and over eight minutes into the film we are presented with our first view of Othello.

The *Cambridge Companion to Shakespeare on Film* (edited by Russell Jackson) includes a wealth of good material, including an article (from which the extract above is taken) by the present author on the films of Orson Welles.

Psychoanalytic criticism

In the twentieth century, psychoanalysis became a major influence on the understanding and interpretation of human behaviour. The founder of psychoanalysis, Sigmund Freud, explained personality as the result of unconscious and irrational desires, repressed memories or wishes, sexuality, fantasy, anxiety and conflict. Inevitably such an approach has been excited by what has been perceived as the psychological complexity of the character, personality and motivations of Iago. Shakespeare was acutely aware of the complexities of human behaviour and, long before Freud, Shakespeare understood the importance of dreams as an embodiment of the unconscious. Iago's invention of Cassio's dream of adultery may provide insight into his own psyche but it might also more directly indicate Iago's awareness of the power of such an experience to provoke a response in a listener such as Othello.

In a play which has as a central concern aspects of sexuality and sexual behaviour it is unsurprising that there has been a great deal of interest in exploring Iago's sexual nature. His misogyny is clear from his early pejorative references to a 'fair wife' and 'spinster' and his abuse of Emilia. Latent homosexuality has been suggested in his attitude towards Othello, and it has been argued as the primary motivation in his desire to control and possess him. The bond they affirm at the end of Act 3 Scene 3 ('Now art thou my lieutenant. / I am your own for ever.') has been seen as a version of the marriage ceremony. Crouched over the collapsed body of Othello after his fit (in Act 4 Scene 1), Iago has been presented as aggressively possessive as he wards off Cassio's attempts to intervene. Such an interpretation has obvious attraction for actors. In 1938, Olivier sought to suggest that his Iago was subconsciously in love with Othello (Ralph Richardson) and had to destroy him. As Othello lay in the clutches of his epilepsy, Iago lay down next to him and simulated an orgasm. Olivier admitted it succeeded only in mystifying the audience at the time. However, in the RSC production in 1985 the relationship between Ben Kingsley's Othello and David Suchet's Iago was undoubtedly influenced by the kind of suppressed homo-eroticism which has been labelled 'the Othello syndrome'.

Organising your responses

The purpose of this section is to help you improve your writing about *Othello*. It offers practical guidance on two kinds of tasks: writing about an extract from the play and writing an essay. Whether you are answering an examination question, preparing coursework or term papers, or carrying out research into your own chosen topic, it is hoped that this section will help you organise and present your responses.

There are two particular considerations which you would do well to keep firmly in mind:

- *Othello* is a play. Although it may be referred to as a 'text', *Othello* is not a book but a script that was written to be acted on a stage. Your response should demonstrate an awareness of the dimension of performance. You need to strive for a theatrical sensitivity, which can be developed ideally by seeing productions in the theatre or by experiencing the play on video or audio-tape. Do seek out more than one interpretation, to avoid your view becoming fixed by a single set of choices. Making the imaginative effort to get the play off the page and visualise ways of staging will help you to write effectively about Shakespeare's language and dramatic techniques.
- *Othello* is not a presentation of 'reality'. It is a dramatic construct in which the playwright engages the emotions and intellect of his theatre audience. The characters and story may persuade an audience to suspend its disbelief for several hours. The audience may identify with the characters, be deeply moved by them, and may think of them as if they were living human beings. However, your task is to show how Shakespeare achieves the dramatic effects that engage an audience. Through discussion of his handling of language, character and situation your writing needs to explore how Shakespeare presents themes and ideas which give insight into social, moral and political issues.

This section offers guidance to help you develop and structure your own ideas. You should feel encouraged to have faith in your own intuitive response. With that as your starting point you can work to establish your own individual style. Curiosity can be your best guide in the early stages and there is much to be said for a degree of humility in approaching the text. Whether setting out on your enquiry or sitting in an exam hall, you should recognise that it is always necessary to spend time thinking what you really want to say. However confident you become in your convictions, you must be wary of sweeping generalisations.

Writing about an extract

Whether or not your study of Shakespeare explicitly requires you to write about an extract from the play, close reading should be regarded as the basis for any interpretative decision. You may be asked to write a detailed commentary upon a passage, or a question may be framed in more specific terms, for example:

> Analyse the style and structure of the extract, showing what it contributes to your appreciation of the play's major concerns.

Perhaps the best advice is to read the passage before you look at the question, remind yourself where it comes in the play and reflect briefly upon its significance. Then read the question very carefully and return to the passage to make some detailed annotation. Check that you are responding to the precise requirements of the question whilst remaining true to your concept of how the passage works. Resist any temptation to tell the story or share ideas that are not specifically required by the question. Only now should you think of beginning to write your response. If you are confronted by a question that lacks specific focus (simply perhaps asking for 'detailed commentary') you might identify and evaluate how the language reveals character, contributes to plot development, offers opportunities for dramatic effect, and embodies crucial concerns of the play as a whole. Such 'crucial concerns' may include the 'themes', 'issues' or 'preoccupations' of the play.

The specific function and quality of any given extract will set its own agenda. There can be no formula that will work for any and every passage. Your priority is to offer the kind of commentary that is essentially true to your experience of the play. Your ideas should be firmly rooted in the text and have the authority conferred by precise and detailed reference. The central thrust of your enquiry should always be to analyse how Shakespeare uses language, assessing the effect of the choices that the playwright has made.

Be clear about the context of the passage and establish some sense of the stage picture. Remember that words may be spoken for the benefit of any member of an on-stage audience or in ignorance of his or her presence. Silent characters can make an important contribution to a scene. Listen, indeed feel, for the pulse of the verse. The emotional temperature may be particularly significant, or perhaps rational debate will predominate. Be prepared to analyse the language in terms not only of the choice of words but also of the way in which they are ordered. Rather than trot out bland generalisations, focus upon the pressure of the dramatic moment and perhaps upon how the relationship between characters is functioning at a particular point. Follow Shakespeare's own advice and 'say what the play treats on, and so grow to a point'.

Extract

Enter OTHELLO

EMILIA   Look where he comes.

DESDEMONA   I will not leave him now; let Cassio
     Be called to him. – How is't with you, my lord?

OTHELLO   Well, my good lady. [*Aside*] O hardness to dissemble!
     How do you, Desdemona?   5

DESDEMONA   Well, my good lord.

OTHELLO   Give me your hand. This hand is moist, my lady.

DESDEMONA   It yet hath felt no age, nor known no sorrow.

OTHELLO   This argues fruitfulness and liberal heart.
     Hot, hot, and moist. This hand of yours requires
     A sequester from liberty, fasting and prayer,   10
     Much castigation, exercise devout;
     For here's a young and sweating devil here
     That commonly rebels. 'Tis a good hand,
     A frank one.

DESDEMONA   You may indeed say so,
     For 'twas that hand that gave away my heart.   15

OTHELLO   A liberal hand! The hearts of old gave hands;
     But our new heraldry is hands, not hearts.

DESDEMONA   I cannot speak of this. Come now, your promise.

OTHELLO   What promise, chuck?

DESDEMONA   I have sent to bid Cassio come speak with you.   20
OTHELLO   I have a salt and sorry rheum offends me;
    Lend me thy handkerchief.
DESDEMONA   Here, my lord.
OTHELLO   That which I gave you.
DESDEMONA   I have it not about me.
OTHELLO   Not?
DESDEMONA   No, faith, my lord.   25
OTHELLO   That's a fault. That handkerchief
    Did an Egyptian to my mother give:
    She was a charmer and could almost read
    The thoughts of people. She told her, while she kept it,
    'Twould make her amiable and subdue my father
    Entirely to her love; but if she lost it   30
    Or made a gift of it, my father's eye
    Should hold her loathèd and his spirits should hunt
    After new fancies. She dying gave it me,
    And bid me when my fate would have me wive,
    To give it her. I did so, and take heed on't: 35
    Make it a darling, like your precious eye.
    To lose't or give't away were such perdition
    As nothing else could match.
DESDEMONA   Is't possible?
OTHELLO   'Tis true. There's magic in the web of it:
    A sibyl, that had numbered in the world   40
    The sun to course two hundred compasses,
    In her prophetic fury sewed the work;
    The worms were hallowed that did breed the silk,
    And it was dyed in mummy, which the skilful
    Conserved of maidens' hearts.   45
DESDEMONA   I'faith, is't true?
OTHELLO   Most veritable; therefore look to't well.
DESDEMONA   Then would to God that I had never seen't!
OTHELLO   Ha? Wherefore?
DESDEMONA   Why do you speak so startingly and rash?
OTHELLO   Is't lost? Is't gone? Speak; is't out of th' way?   50
DESDEMONA   Heaven bless us!
OTHELLO   Say you?
DESDEMONA   It is not lost, but what and if it were?

OTHELLO   How?

DESDEMONA   I say it is not lost.   55

OTHELLO   Fetch't, let me see't.

DESDEMONA   Why so I can, sir; but I will not now.

This is a trick to put me from my suit.

Pray you let Cassio be received again.

OTHELLO   Fetch me the handkerchief. My mind misgives.

DESDEMONA   Come, come;   60

You'll never meet a more sufficient man.

OTHELLO   The handkerchief!

DESDEMONA   I pray, talk me of Cassio.

OTHELLO   The handkerchief!

DESDEMONA   A man that all his time

Hath founded his good fortunes on your love,

Shared dangers with you –   65

OTHELLO   The handkerchief!

DESDEMONA   I'faith, you are to blame.

OTHELLO   Zounds!   *Exit*

[*Act 3 Scene 4, lines 27–93*]

In preparing to write about an extract try to imagine how the action might be staged but remember that there can be various ways of performing a scene that may be equally valid. If appropriate, offer alternatives but justify your own preferences by close and detailed reference to the text. Do pay attention to Shakespeare's implicit stage directions and be prepared to consider how strongly the emblematic use of props can read. Throughout your analysis keep in mind the sense of audience, both in terms of characters on stage and in terms of how the sympathies or intellectual judgement of the theatre-going public are engaged. Seek to make your points concisely and do not waste words in repetition.

Example

The passage occurs shortly after the 'temptation' scene (Act 3 Scene 3) and brings Othello and Desdemona together for the first time after he has become convinced of her infidelity. She has just shared with Emilia her concern about the missing handkerchief. Emilia has curiously denied knowledge of its whereabouts.

Emilia signals Othello's entrance, allowing a moment for

Desdemona and the audience to prepare for the encounter. Desdemona expresses her resolution in a simplistic, almost childlike manner, confident of her influence over her husband. Referring to Cassio here serves to remind an audience of how successfully Iago has created suspicion in Othello's mind. The elision that is necessary in 'How is't with you?' indicates Desdemona's rapid and impulsive enthusiasm, which is reined back by the deferential formality of 'my lord'. There is a disturbing, even ominous, ambivalence in the single word he gives her by way of response before he echoes her formal style of address with the insertion of 'good'. For an audience with privileged knowledge of his agenda the word carries a weight of meaning. It is her goodness which he is here to interrogate.

An editor has taken the interpretative decision to mark Othello's comment, 'O hardness to dissemble!', as an aside. It is not addressed to anyone on stage but it expresses a pressure of feeling and the conflict within Othello. The dichotomy between a sense of 'self' and 'other self' is described in *Antony and Cleopatra* as the hero's 'divided disposition' and the phrase is relevant here. Othello's struggle is between an emotional faith in his marital bond and a supposedly rational judgement that he is being deceived. Desdemona had earlier recognised that there can be a social, self-protective imperative to mask one's true feelings:

> I am not merry, but I do beguile
> The thing I am by seeming otherwise

> *(Act 2 Scene 1, lines 121–2)*

Her observation sheds light upon the complexity of the misapprehension, misunderstanding and deception which characterises the action of the play. People naturally, and at times appropriately, 'dissemble'. It is not only villainy which exploits a disparity between appearance and motivation, for the theatrical experience itself involves an appreciation of an actor's skill in dissembling.

Othello necessarily turns away from his wife and then back to her for the resonant solemnity of 'How do you, Desdemona?' Whether playfully, anxiously, or because she is aware of Emilia's presence, she now matches quite precisely the ponderous propriety of his reply. At the very least this suggests that she has registered an oddness in his manner. Her response to his request for her hand is silent, immediate and unquestioning. His patterned repetition of 'hand', coupled with an alliterative 'm', expresses the emblem of partnership whilst also indicating an investment of personal feeling. He had, of course, asked for her hand once before, but in addition to a reminder of the marriage service there may be a striking parallel with the alliance Othello has just forged with Iago. At the end of the previous scene Iago surrendered:

> The execution of his wit, hands, heart,
> To wronged Othello's service.   *(Act 3 Scene 3, lines 467–8)*

In reading Desdemona's palm Othello changes the relationship between them. When he examines her hand his language yokes a religious absolutism of 'fasting and prayer' and 'castigation, exercise devout' with the fiercely sensual physicality of 'fruitfulness', 'moist' and 'young and sweating'. Othello is establishing himself as a figure of authority and judgement, which invests the whole act of reading her palm with foreboding. 'Hand' is set against 'heart' and the insistent juxtaposition of the words prompts a recognition that Othello's allegiance has changed. He is now giving priority to the badge by which a man is known, his public persona. His words are turning back upon themselves with the agony of his inner debate mirrored in the repetitions. His commitment is to the imperative of a notion of honour, reflected in 'our new heraldry is hands, not hearts'. The triteness of the alliteration suggests that this is some new mantra with which he is consoling himself. His bond with Desdemona has been superseded by his partnership with Iago.

Desdemona is bewildered by his riddling and returns to her mission, cajoling her husband to think of an earlier promise. Just briefly, Othello lapses into his former affectionate indulgence, 'What promise, chuck?' Desdemona's explicit reference to Cassio prompts a discontinuity in the dialogue. Othello's sudden assertion of a 'salt and sorry rheum' is not so much clumsy evasion as the transparent initiation of a process of testing. It should scarcely matter which handkerchief, and Desdemona's response to his clipped urgency is an implicit recognition that the request is invested with significance. She nervously avoids admitting that she has mislaid her handkerchief but the way in which she casts round for an excuse is a virtual admission that she has lost it, 'I have it not about me.'

When she offers a substitute handkerchief, she apparently provides Othello with 'ocular proof' of her infidelity. In Sergei Yutkevich's film (1955), Othello is looking away and closes his hand round the piece of cloth in relief as he tenderly embraces Desdemona. When he subsequently realises that it is not the handkerchief 'spotted with strawberries' that was 'his first gift' to her, his reaction is to throw it from him angrily. The sequence effectively demonstrates how the substituted handkerchief can be seen by Othello to represent the way in which he believes Cassio has replaced him in Desdemona's affections.

Othello invests the handkerchief with mystical power to bolster its significance. He invents an account of its history which is different from the version he will offer in the last scene of the play. Later (in Act 5 Scene 2) the more mundane claim is that 'My father gave my mother' the handkerchief. Here, the supposed involvement of an 'Egyptian', a 'charmer', is combined with a tidal, incantatory power to suggest supernatural forces at work. Othello's fervour is reflected in the surging enjambement and he seems almost to convince himself of some immense symbolic significance. He claims an inherited responsibility to promote his own sense of being an instrument of divine retribution. He astonishingly asserts that the simple act of losing a handkerchief is equivalent to 'perdition', the condemnation of a soul to eternal damnation.

Desdemona can only gasp in astonishment, which parallels her reported response to Othello when he first came 'a-wooing'. Othello spins his own web of words to evoke a world of myth and fantastic ritual. His extraordinary account of the 'sibyl' sewing in 'prophetic fury' with silk from 'hallowed' worms becomes quite gruesomely macabre. It can be no more than another traveller's tale but it works its spell on Desdemona.

Following Othello's sustained speeches, the single or incomplete lines quicken the pulse and suggest how Othello's conviction and Desdemona's anxiety are increasing. Her utterances disintegrate into expressions of anger, fear, incomprehension and distress as she tries to talk about Cassio, despite Othello reiterating his questions about the handkerchief. Othello has lost faith in his intuitive response to Desdemona as he has been guided by Iago to believe that women habitually deceive. He will not let himself trust in her apparent truthfulness and honesty. When she insists, 'It is not lost', she is affirming an essential truth. If the handkerchief symbolises mutual fidelity and love then indeed it is not lost. Her repetition of 'I say it is not lost' is also touchingly human.

The gulf between husband and wife is signalled as their words clash against each other in a rapid exchange. Desdemona cannot be expected to realise how her words will be interpreted. From her perspective, Othello's mood has changed since he dismissed Cassio. Understandably she assumes that healing the rift with a man who 'Hath founded his good fortunes on your love' and who was instrumental in assisting their courtship will restore the marital harmony. Her best efforts to re-establish the bond with her husband work (thanks to Iago) to destroy it. Throughout this passage Desdemona is sympathetically and realistically presented. Her distress ultimately gives way to frustration when she states, 'I'faith, you are to blame.' Othello cannot see beyond the absence of 'the handkerchief', repeating the phrase over and over again. Words become inadequate to express his frustration and sense of betrayal and he leaves the stage with an exasperated 'Zounds!'

Emilia's only words in the passage, 'Look where he comes', are a precise echo of her husband's words in the previous scene (line 331). This confirms the bond between them which has caused Emilia to lie to Desdemona about the handkerchief. An audience will inevitably be interested in Emilia's silent reaction. She might retreat to allow it to be a more private scene but Shakespeare did not choose to have her leave the stage, which implies that an audience should see her listen to the conversation between Othello and Desdemona. She might be given some stage business to provide her with a cover for what might be construed as awkwardness or shame. Taking refuge in sewing would provide a counterpart to Othello's words about the sibyl and would be ironic in a scene of disintegration. Zoë Wanamaker's Emilia (for the Royal Shakespeare Company at The Other Place in 1989) registered a kind of pained satisfaction that the beautiful, fortunate Desdemona was, for once, experiencing some of the marital discord that was habitual for Emilia.

This passage demonstrates how the trust between Othello and Desdemona is destroyed by Othello's conviction of her infidelity. It makes clear how he has been able to convince himself, despite any 'ocular proof'. A misplaced handkerchief is fulfilling Iago's prediction that such 'trifles' can become 'confirmations strong / As proofs of holy writ'. At this point Othello has no evidence except uncorroborated assertion from Iago and the circumstantial loss of the handkerchief. It is a disturbing episode because it demonstrates the impossibility of Desdemona's innocence being believed. Emilia's presence in the scene is a constant reminder of the truth of the whereabouts of the handkerchief and of Iago's manipulative power. Her silent observation may be disconcerting but will ultimately inspire her passionate defence of her mistress in the final scene. Her silence will be replaced by an authoritative, courageous and determined fluency to ensure that the truth is revealed.

Writing an essay

There is no panacea for contending with the rigours of essay-writing. No universal pattern, fixed structure or magic formula will substitute for grappling with the material yourself and taking decisions about the approach that will best suit a particular task. Different strategies are appropriate to different people on different occasions. Uniformity of approach would be deadly dull and would stifle individuality. The notion that essay-writing skills are 'caught' and not 'taught' should encourage you to read widely and develop your own style. Studying critical writing is a stimulating way of prompting ideas, extending your own thoughts or offering you a sounding board on which to test opinions. However, the process of absorbing how others present ideas can be as valuable as engaging with the ideas themselves. You should feel encouraged to develop a distinctive voice whilst recognising that your essays need a clear line of argument and a firm sense of direction. Your aim should be to seek to persuade the reader of the validity of your ideas on the play. Crucially you need to answer the question, selecting details that are relevant and demonstrating an informed and intelligent response to the text. Quotations must earn their keep. There is no merit in copying out slabs of text – select what is pertinent, directing your reader's attention to those particular aspects of diction, syntax, rhythm, etc. which serve your argument.

You can write about *Othello* from different points of view and you will write better if you have faith in your argument. Do take every opportunity to test your ideas in discussion. It is worth reiterating how useful it can be to watch and/or listen to a fresh interpretation. Although stage productions may be few and far between these days, there are more than 20 audio and video versions, making comparisons of *Othello* in performance readily accessible (see pages 127–8). The better you know the play the more readily you will recognise that simply telling the story or describing characters is comparatively worthless. Analysing events or characters must inevitably prompt engagement with the wider concerns of the play. In *Othello* these include the issue of race, the relationships within marriage, the conflict between public duty and private concerns, the importance of reputation, the pressures of ambition, attitudes towards love and loyalty, etc.

Example

> '*Othello* is merely a tragedy of misunderstanding.' Discuss.

The word 'merely' should ring alarm bells. By the time you take an examination or even write your first essay on *Othello* you should know the play well enough and have sufficient respect for its complexity to resist the suggestion that it might be reduced to a 'mere' anything. You should recognise at the outset that you are being given an opportunity to say what you think is the scope of the play and what it achieves. You do need, however, to engage with the particular frame of the question and must engage with the inherent contradiction in the notion that 'misunderstanding' can provoke 'tragedy'. You might therefore begin by considering very briefly notions of Aristotelian theory and the notion of a tragic flaw. You should quickly establish how 'misunderstanding' trivialises the play. Rymer (see pages 90–1) might be useful here. You then have scope to take your essay in one of several directions.

The personal tragedy of Othello

- Othello's sense of racial superiority and his pride in Desdemona; importance of relocation to Cyprus; no role for Othello; his insecurity compounded by new setting and difficulty in reconciling military and personal dimensions
- his responsiveness to suggestion; need for certainty, 'to be once in doubt / Is once to be resolved'; importance of reputation and the element of self-dramatisation, 'Othello's occupation's gone'; bond

- with Iago resulting in a commitment to a pattern of supposedly rational behaviour; suppression of intuitive emotional response; power of imagination to make any 'ocular proof' unnecessary; consideration of the arguments used by Bradley and Leavis
- disintegration into epileptic fit; humiliation of hiding to overhear; conviction of the moral imperative in 'yet she must die'; seeing himself as an 'honourable murderer'
- grief at realisation of what he has done; courage, self-awareness and clarity of judgement in final speech, 'Set you down this', 'one that loved not wisely, but too well'; Othello's concept of judicial execution; tribute offered by Cassio, 'he was great of heart'

A tragedy of failure in personal relationships

- small group of characters, tightly held by intertwining relationships: military, domestic, marital allegiances
- everyone trusts Iago; Roderigo's friendship masks the reality of exploitation; tensions between Iago and Cassio; peer-group pressure in drinking scene; Montano's respect for Iago and doubts about Cassio; Othello's insistence upon military discipline and the need to make an example of Cassio, 'Cassio, I love thee, / But never more be officer of mine'
- Brabantio unable to come to terms with his daughter's marriage; clarity of her argument about transfer of allegiance from father to husband; pain of Brabantio's loss, proving fatal; Othello's references to his parents; Desdemona's memory of her mother's relationship with her maid, Barbary
- three women in failed relationships of love and commitment; Desdemona's unconditional love for Othello, 'Whate'er you be, I am obedient'; Emilia's willingness to lie for her husband; Bianca's loyalty and concern for Cassio whom she hopes to marry; the 'tragic loading of this bed' includes Emilia – double significance of 'he hath killed his wife'

A tragedy of social intolerance

- issue of race is central to the play, patterned in the juxtaposition of night and day; symbolic function of black and white
- conflict between public and private roles; Othello accepted because of his status and importance as a military figure in Venice; his

'otherness' exposes racial tensions in Venice; opposition of Brabantio to marriage; political pragmatism of Duke's decision

- Othello's insecurity and inexperience in social world; lack of understanding of differences in 'climate, complexion and degree'; Iago able to exploit social isolation
- Venetian attitudes towards women; Brabantio's patriarchal stance; Duke's assumption that Desdemona will return home while Othello goes to Cyprus; women seen as 'virgin' or 'whore'; attitudes towards Bianca, whose cry 'I am no strumpet' goes unheard
- re-establishment of control through Lodovico; irony of 'Cassio shall have my place'; Lodovico's frustrated determination to arrest Othello and put him on trial; no sense of Venetian society having learned from the experience; bleak picture of the future with prospect of torture for Iago, and Othello's words, 'I'd have thee live, / For in my sense 'tis happiness to die'

The approaches outlined above should not be regarded as prescriptive, exhaustive or mutually exclusive. You should combine material in a way that reflects what you determine to be the priorities. The best essays will have an organic development. Inevitably there must be a process of selection but you should not let a flood of ideas erode the need for precise and detailed reference. Keep quotations brief (one or two words will often suffice) and ensure that you do not lose sight of the question.

In the case of this particular question you could usefully conclude by considering the impact of the way in which the play ends. You might offer something along the following lines:

> In the final moments of the play an audience is prompted to 'Look on the tragic loading of this bed', which is a tableau that contains not only the bodies of Othello and Desdemona but also that of Emilia. While Othello's tragedy dominates the play, the emotional power of the story is intensified by the sacrifice of so many other characters too. Desdemona, Emilia and Brabantio are all victims. There is a sense of death as a reconciliation for Othello and Desdemona but also a desperate sense of terrible waste in the destruction of so remarkable an emotional commitment as existed between Othello and Desdemona.

Writing about character

Much critical writing about *Othello* traditionally focused on characters, writing about them as if they were living human beings. Today you are expected to understand that they are theatrical constructs serving a dramatic function. They embody the wider concerns of the play and exist only while they are on stage in a social and political world with defined values and beliefs.

Tracing each character's journey through the play, as an actor or actress does, is a useful way of engaging with the role, rather than simply with the character. To establish which scenes a particular character is in and the distribution of his or her lines enables you to look at the 'part'. In Shakespeare's day, the actors were given not a copy of the whole play but simply their own lines, written out with just the cues to help them in rehearsal. In *A Midsummer Night's Dream*, Snug is very upset that he is not given a script because the lion's part is nothing but roaring which he can do 'extempore'.

Working through the text from the perspective of each character is a way of turning the play round to look at it from the inside. Such an exercise sheds light on how it is structured. What takes place away from the centre of the action may make an important contribution to the thematic debate or to the impact of the play in performance. Looking at Roderigo in this way reveals that he is absent from the action during Act 3 and when he reappears he is less easy to manipulate. He challenges Iago and puts pressure upon him. His threat to ask Desdemona to return his money and jewels forces Iago to improvise. Roderigo has the potential to reveal the truth about Iago – indeed that potential existed at the beginning of the play, though it may be that an audience only appreciates that ability in Act 4. In addition to his structural importance, he contributes to the play's exploration of how love shapes behaviour. Roderigo is made vulnerable, insecure and desperate by his love. He is one of the suitors Desdemona rejected but, rather than assume that he is unattractive and stupid, it could be stimulating to cast him as a courtly suitor in the tradition of Paris (in *Romeo and Juliet*) rather than as 'a coxcomb . . . a thin-faced knave, a gull' like Sir Andrew Aguecheek (in *Twelfth Night*). Simplistic assessment of character condemns Roderigo as naive and foolish, with more money than sense. This undervalues Iago's skill and it is useful to remember that Shakespeare invented Roderigo. He has no counterpart in Cinthio's narrative and that should be further incentive to investigate his contribution to the play.

Shakespeare invites comparisons between characters as a primary means of evaluation. Roderigo lacks the qualities of poise, eloquence and assurance that Cassio has in abundance. However, members of an audience may come to regard those qualities with suspicion, but initially they are unlikely to want to share Iago's jealousy and dislike of Cassio and are more likely to endorse Othello's faith in him. Yet, whereas Roderigo will sell all his land to follow his heart, Cassio is determinedly ambitious and concerned above all with his reputation. Although he is having an active sexual relationship with Bianca (who he acknowledges loves him) he does not wish Othello to see him 'womaned' and he chooses not to marry her.

At the end of the play the stage picture invites comparison between Cassio and Iago as the two injured men are juxtaposed. Cassio has had his leg cut almost in two and Iago says, 'I bleed, sir, but not killed.' Cassio now rules in Cyprus and has Iago at his mercy. The man Iago described so sharply as 'this counter-caster', who had 'never set a squadron in the field', has triumphed. He has been careful to protect a reputation badly tarnished by his drunkenness and yet skilfully rebuilt by exploiting all three women in the play.

Cassio is a man who Othello declared 'went between us very oft'. Perhaps he secured his military appointment in the first place as a public reward for private service. He loses it through his own inadequacy, indiscipline and a self-acknowledged weakness. He sought to get his job back by, once again, going between Othello and Desdemona, now taking advantage of Desdemona's understandable sense of personal indebtedness. He uses Emilia and he treats Bianca with contempt. Careful study of the ways in which the women are linked in the play may shed new light upon Cassio. Traditionally he has shouldered no responsibility for the success of Iago's plot, but looking at him through the perspectives offered by the women and by means of comparison with the other men makes him more complex and less straightforward than he might initially appear.

Looking at the trio of women together can open up areas of interest both structurally and thematically. The handkerchief is important for all of them in their relationships with the men they love, and although traditionally it is the differences between the women that have interested critics there are important similarities between them. The changes Shakespeare made to his source in relation to the role of Bianca emphasises her contribution to the play's exploration of relationships. Not only is she like Desdemona and Emilia in her commitment to the man she loves, but like Roderigo her love makes her vulnerable.

The importance of a character cannot simply be judged by reference to the number of words the dramatist has provided. Seemingly minor roles carry significant weight. The Duke makes clear Othello's importance to the state of Venice and the political imperatives which take precedence over Brabantio's private concerns. The Duke's respect for Othello explains Brabantio's willingness to entertain Othello but that social acceptance is challenged by the elopement. Characteristically, Shakespeare humanises Brabantio, allowing an audience to understand, but not condone, his prejudice. The way in which events in the senate scene unfold makes clear the tensions inherent in collisions of culture. Brabantio's warning to Othello that a daughter who deceives her father could deceive her husband forges a terrible and tragic link between the two men, who both die unable to survive their loss of Desdemona.

Consideration of the characters of Othello and Iago can still usefully take as its starting point an examination of the opposing views offered by Bradley and Leavis (see pages 91–3). Enquiry into ideas about tragedy may stimulate thinking, but what is crucially important is the process of close reading to test competing theories. The modern interest in psychological inquiry has revived enthusiasm for Bradley's interest in Iago, but the balance of the play can be restored not merely by studying Leavis' argument but by more fundamentally experiencing the play in the theatre or by means of the range of available recordings (see pages 127–8). Intellectual fascination with the seeming complexities of Iago is matter for the study rather than the stage. The emotional impact of Othello's tragedy can be lacerating in performance.

A note on examiners

Examiners are kindly men and women who are delighted when they have scripts to mark that are lively and show real engagement with the text. They struggle to set questions which are not amenable to the prepared stock essay but which (they hope) will stimulate candidates to write vigorously and enthusiastically. A careful, detailed knowledge of the text should be the springboard for a vigorous engagement with the precise demands of a particular question. Students must be prepared to select from all they might wish to say only what is strictly pertinent to the question the examiners do ask, rather than tackle the question that it was forlornly hoped would be asked! Quotations should never be merely decorative. They give life to an essay and provide the evidence which clinches the argument.

The pressure of an examination can make its own contribution to the process of exploration and discovery. Whilst it is desirable that the opening sentences of your response signal a clear sense of direction, it is often the case that ideas develop during the course of an essay. However, some recognition of any such shift should be signalled in the concluding sentences. The value of critical reading has been argued throughout this book. Fortunately, the days of learning critical gobbets off by heart to impress the examiners are long gone. It remains important that credit for a particular idea (whether it is endorsed or refuted) is fairly attributed, but the overriding priority is for students to forge their own responses.

Resources

Books

Although some of these books are out of print all of them are available in or through college libraries.

Jane Adamson, *'Othello' as Tragedy: Some Problems of Judgement and Feeling*, Cambridge University Press, 1980

Catherine M S Alexander & Stanley Wells (eds.), *Shakespeare and Race*, Cambridge University Press, 2000

Antony Gerard Barthelemy, *Black Face, Maligned Race: The Representation of Blacks in English Drama from Shakespeare to Southerne*, Louisiana State University Press, 1987

A C Bradley, *Shakespearean Tragedy*, Macmillan, 1904; 2nd edition, 1905 *

John Russell Brown, *Shakespeare's Plays in Performance*, Edward Arnold, 1966

Peter Davison, *The Critics' Debate: 'Othello'*, Macmillan, 1988

T S Eliot, 'Shakespeare and the Stoicism of Seneca' (1927) in *Selected Essays*, Faber, 1932, 126–40 *

William Empson, *The Structure of Complex Words*, Chatto and Windus, 1951 *

Evelyn Gajowski, 'The Female Perspective in *Othello*' in Virginia Mason Vaughan & Kent Cartwright (eds.), *'Othello': New Perspectives*, Fairleigh Dickinson Press, New Jersey, 1981

Harley Granville Barker, *Prefaces to Shakespeare: Love's Labour's Lost, Romeo and Juliet, The Merchant of Venice, Othello*, Batsford, 1930; illustrated edition, 1963

Eamon Grennan, 'The Women's Voices in *Othello*: Speech, Song, Silence' in *Shakespeare Quarterly 38* (1987), 275–92

Julie Hankey, *Plays in Performance: Othello*, Bristol Classical Press, 1987

Terence Hawkes (ed.), *Coleridge on Shakespeare*, Penguin, 1969

E A J Honigmann, *The Texts of 'Othello' and Shakespearian Revision*, Routledge, 1996

Russell Jackson (ed.), *The Cambridge Companion to Shakespeare on Film*, Cambridge University Press, 2000

G Wilson Knight, *The Wheel of Fire*, Oxford University Press, 1930 *

F R Leavis, 'Diabolic Intellect and the Noble Hero' in *Scrutiny, 6* (1937), 259–83; reprinted in his *The Common Pursuit*, Chatto and Windus, 1952, 136–59 *

Micheál MacLiammóir, *Put Money in thy Purse: The Filming of Orson Welles's 'Othello'*, Methuen, 1952

B H de Mendonca, '*Othello*: A Tragedy Built on a Comic Structure', in *Shakespeare Survey 21* (1968), 31–8

Karen Newman, '"And Wash the Ethiop White": Femininity and the Monstrous in "Othello"', in Jean E Howard and Marian F O'Connor (eds.), *Shakespeare Reproduced: The Text in History and Ideology*, Routledge, 1987, 143–62

Laurence Olivier, *On Acting*, Weidenfeld & Nicolson, 1986

Keith Parsons & Pamela Mason (eds.), *Shakespeare in Performance*, Salamander Books, 1995

Marvin Rosenberg, *The Masks of 'Othello'*, University of Delaware Press, 1961

Thomas Rymer, 'A Short View of Tragedy, London, 1693' in J E Spingarn (ed.), *Critical Essays of the Seventeenth Century*, Clarendon Press, 1908, Vol II, 221–48 *

T J B Spencer (ed.), *Elizabethan Love Stories*, Penguin, 1968

Caroline Spurgeon, *Shakespeare's Imagery and What it Tells Us*, Cambridge University Press, 1935

Kenneth Tynan, *Othello: The National Theatre Production*, Rupert Hart-Davis Ltd, 1966

Virginia Mason Vaughan, *'Othello': A Contextual History*, Cambridge University Press, 1994

Stanley Wells, *Shakespeare: A Dramatic Life*, Methuen, 1994

W K Wimsatt (ed.), *Dr Johnson on Shakespeare*, Penguin, 1969 *

Martin L Wine, *Text and Performance: 'Othello'*, Macmillan, 1984

* These articles (or extracts from them) are included in John Wain (ed.), *'Othello': A Casebook*, Macmillan, 1971

Screen versions of *Othello*

1922   Wörner-Film, directed by Dmitri Buchowetzki
Emil Jannings, Werner Kraus, Ica von Lenkeffy, Lya de Putti
– a silent German Expressionist film available with English titles.

1952   Mercury, directed by Orson Welles
Orson Welles, Micheál MacLiammóir, Suzanne Cloutier, Fay Compton
– an immensely powerful performance which has stood the test of time.

1955   Mosfilm, directed by Sergei Yutkevich
Sergei Bondarchuk, Andrei Popov, Irina Skobtseva, A Maximova
– visually striking in its emblematic use of nets, tidal forces, etc.

1965   BHE (National Theatre production), directed by Stuart Burge
Laurence Olivier, Frank Finlay, Maggie Smith, Joyce Redman
– a remarkable record of a supremely great stage performance.

1981   Shakespeare Collection, directed by Franklin Melton
William Marshall, Ron Moody, Jenny Agutter, Leslie Paxton
– the play's theatricality is thwarted by the television vocabulary.

1981   BBC-TV, directed by Jonathan Miller
Anthony Hopkins, Bob Hoskins, Penelope Wilton, Rosemary Leach
– the domestic frame has difficulty in accommodating a manic Iago.

1988   Market Theatre of Johannesburg, directed by Janet Suzman
John Kani, Richard Haddon Haines, Joanna Weinberg, Dorothy Gould
– Afrikaner attitudes are examined in the immediate aftermath of apartheid.

1990   Primetime (RSC production), directed by Trevor Nunn
Willard White, Ian McKellen, Imogen Stubbs, Zoë Wanamaker
– fascinating in its study of Emilia's relationship with her husband.

1996   Castle Rock, directed by Oliver Parker
Laurence Fishburne, Kenneth Branagh, Irène Jacob, Anna Warwick
– moves away from the stage to create the forced intimacy of an erotic thriller.

Screen adaptations

1947   *A Double Life*, directed by George Cukor
Ronald Colman, Edmond O'Brien, Signe Hasso, Shelley Winters
– an intriguing thriller built upon an interplay between performance and reality.

1956   *Jubal*, directed by Delmer Daves
Glenn Ford [as 'Cassio'], Ernest Borgnine, Rod Steiger, Valerie French
– sultry 'Desdemona' is jealous of virtuous 'Bianca's' influence upon 'Cassio'.

1973	*Catch My Soul*, directed by Patrick McGoohan
	Richie Havens, Lance Le Gault, Season Hubley, Susan Tyrrell
	– the film version of Jack Gold's rock musical.
1974	Verdi's *Otello*, directed by Herbert von Karajan
	John Vickers, Peter Glossop, Mirella Freni, Stefania Malagú
	– filmed on location with an inevitable collision between naturalism
	and operatic convention.
1992	Verdi's *Otello*, directed by Elijah Moshinsky
	Placido Domingo, Sergei Leiferkus, Kiri Te Kanawa, Claire Powell
	– as staged at the Royal Opera House with the scenes between Othello and
	Desdemona especially thrilling.

Sound recordings

1944	Pearl Plays and Poets
	Paul Robeson, Jose Ferrer, Uta Hagen, Edith King
1957	Argo, directed by George Rylands
	Tony Church, Donald Beves, Wendy Gifford, Irene Worth
1961	Living Shakespeare, directed by Michael Benthall
	John Gielgud, Ralph Richardson, Barbara Jefford, Coral Browne
1962	Harper Collins (formerly Caedmon), directed by Howard Sackler
	Frank Silvera, Cyril Cusack, Anna Massey, Celia Johnson
1971	Argo, directed by George Rylands
	Richard Johnson, Ian Holm, Anna Calder-Marshall, Peggy Ashcroft
1983	BBC Radio
	Paul Scofield, Nicol Williamson, Hannah Gordon, Rosalind Shanks
2000	Arkangel, directed by Clive Brill
	Don Warrington, David Threlfall, Anne-Marie Duff, Suzanne Bertish
2000	Naxos, directed by David Timson
	Hugh Quarshie, Anton Lesser, Emma Fielding, Patience Tomlinson

Casting above is listed as follows: Othello, Iago, Desdemona, Emilia.